HISTORICAL WOMEN OF NORFOLK

MICHAEL CHANDLER

AMBERLEY

Dedicated to Ross

First published 2016

Amberley Publishing
The Hill, Stroud
Gloucestershire, GL5 4EP

www.amberley-books.com

Copyright © Michael Chandler, 2016

Photographs © Michael Chandler, 2016

The right of Michael Chandler to be identified
as the Author of this work has been asserted in
accordance with the Copyrights, Designs and
Patents Act 1988.

ISBN 978 1 4456 5322 8 (print)
ISBN 978 1 4456 5323 5 (ebook)

British Library Cataloguing in Publication Data.
A catalogue record for this book is available from
the British Library.

Typesetting by Amberley Publishing.
Printed in the UK.

ACKNOWLEDGEMENTS

Thanks to Archant, Cassie Ulph, Cavell Nurses' Trust, the D-Day and Normandy Fellowship, Eastern Counties Newspapers, James E. Broughton, Norfolk Record Office, Norfolk and Norwich Millennium Library, Rosemary Dixon, *Great Yarmouth Mercury* and Wymondham Heritage Museum.

FOREWORD

Historical Women of Norfolk by Michael Chandler, who has an understanding of Norfolk and Norwich history through his writing of previous books, has put together this collection of incredible stories of women who made their mark not only in the county of Norfolk, but also around the world.

For those of you looking to learn more about historical facts of certain women in the county, this book has to be your first port of call. You will learn historical facts about women such as the actress Charlotte Atkyns, resident of Kettering Hall, who spent all her money trying to free Marie Antoinette, and Mable Clarkson, who became the first woman in council chamber at Norwich City Hall, to Phillipa Flowerday, who was appointed the first-ever industrial nurse and was employed by Colman's Mustard. Other women mentioned include Kitty Higdon and her husband Tom, who were part of the longest-lasting strike ever at a school; Dr Joyce M. Lambert, who discovered that the Norfolk Broads were man-made; and Anna Sewell, the author of the novel *Black Beauty*.

These are just a few of the names included; in fact there is a host of unforgettable women who have made history in the county of Norfolk, and I am sure that this book will give pleasure to those who will read it and students who will hopefully learn from its many stories.

The Duchess of Norfolk, 2016

CONTENTS

Introduction

INTRODUCTION

This book aims to cover some of the historical women of Norfolk, whose contributions have been enormous; indeed, we have just paid tribute to Edith Cavell, who was executed 100 years ago.

When visiting the wonderful county of Norfolk you are visiting an area of outstanding beauty that many heroines from history have walked on; for example Boadicea, who was the Queen of the Iceni people, was born close to Norwich near the River Wensum.

There will be many names that you recognised, but also many surprises. I'm sure the majority of you have seen the film *The Sound of Music* and sing along to the tune 'Do- Re-Mi', but did you know this was written by Sarah Glover of Norwich, was called the Norwich Sol-fa notation and was sung by children at Sunday school.

It was in Norwich that Dame Julian wrote her sixteen *Revelations of Divine Love*. There was the actress Charlotte Atkyns who was also known as the female Scarlet Pimpernel, who tried to free Marie Antoinette. Charlotte and her husband lived in Ketteringham Hall near Wymondham.

Children's classic *Black Beauty* was written in Old Catton by Anna Sewell. Social reformer Elizabeth Fry was born not far from Anglia Square. A member of the Quaker Gurney family, she has been seen on the back of the UK five-pound note.

Great authors and thinkers such as Amelia Opie and Harriet Martineau have, and rightly so, made a big impact in Norfolk and around the world, along with Margery Kempe, author of the earliest surviving autobiography in English, and Anna Gurney, who was the first female member of the British Archaeological Society. Also included is the story of the Burston school strike and England's first female mayoress, Ethel Colman.

Some of what has been achieved is groundbreaking, such as Dr Joyce M. Lambert who discovered that the Broads were man-made, but received no recommendation for this; Philippa Flowerday, who became the first industrial nurse situated at Colman's; and Margaret Fountaine, whose collection of 22,000 butterflies is housed at the Norwich Castle Museum.

There are also some unsavoury stories to tell, such as the story of Mother Gabley from King's Lynn, who was hanged for witchcraft, and that of Elizabeth Cooper, who was burnt at the stake at Lollards Pit for interrupting a service at St Andrew's in Norwich.

Alicia Meynell became the first female jockey to beat a male jockey; Doreen Wallace became a prolific author, publishing fifty-four books from 1918 to the 1970s; and Ann Drummond became the first person to be buried at the Rosary Cemetery in Norwich.

I have even included some influential women who were not born in Norfolk but spent time in the county, such as ecologist Marietta Pallis, Mabel Clarkson (the first female sheriff of Norwich), and Swedish opera singer Jenny Lind, whose concerts for the Bishop of Norwich helped set up a children's hospital which today forms part of the Norfolk and Norwich University Hospital.

I have been truly inspired by the number of influential women that I have researched for this book and it is with such strong apologies and with a heavy heart that I am not able to include more fascinating stories.

Michael Chandler
Norwich, 2016

Aitken, (Marion) Violet (1886–1987)

Marion was the daughter of Canon W. H. M. H. (Hay) Aitken who was positioned at Norwich Cathedral. Marion was a suffragette prisoner and hunger striker who was employed as a full-time worker for the suffragettes. She was born on 21 January 1886 in Bedford and died in November 1987 aged 101 in Hertfordshire. Her father's diary entry of 5 March 1912 states that she has been again arrested and this time for breaking a plate glass:

> I am overwhelmed with shame a distress to think that a daughter of mine should do anything so wicked … But my poor wife! It's heart breaking to think of her being exposed in her old age to the horror… God Help us!

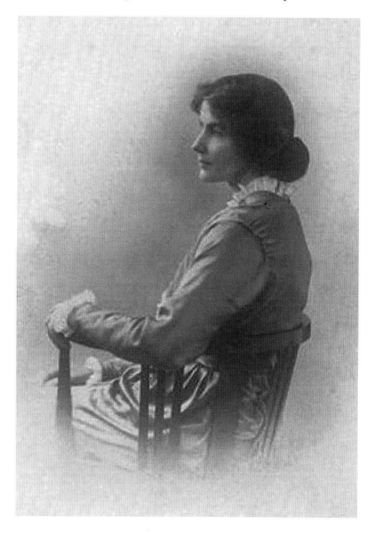

(Marion) Violet Aitken.

Violet also appeared on the roll of honour of suffragette prisoners 1905–14, the record of which is held by the London School of Economics Women's Library. On 15 March 1912, Violet, along with Miss Clara Given, were fined £100 for breaking twelve windows at Jays Ltd, 245 Regent Street, London.

Atkyns, Charlotte (1758–1836)

Charlotte Atkyns (*née* Walpole) born in County Westmeath, Ireland, was a British actress related to Prime Minister Robert Walpole. She made her stage debut as Leonora in *The Padlock* by Isaac Bickerstaff at the Crow Street Theatre in Dublin. She made her London debut at Drury Lane on 2 October 1777 playing Rosetta in Bickerstaffe's *Love in a Village*, for which she received the sum of £4 per week and a further £48 5s for her benefit on the 1 May 1778. After this, Charlotte spent the summer at Bath before returning to Drury Lane for the 1778/79 season, and after this period she married Sir Edward Atkyns of Ketteringham Hall, the grandson of a Lord Chief Justice, and they moved to France. Because of Charlotte's pedigree and background it meant that the Norfolk gentry of Ketteringham never accepted her. They had two sons, Edward, who died on 27 March 1794 aged thirty-six, and Wright Edward, born in 1780, who would later become a captain in the First Royals.

They settled at Ketteringham Hall before moving to France in November 1784, where they entered court circles at Versailles. They returned to Ketteringham in 1791 and Charlotte extended her contacts for French émigrés, the most important being the journalist Jean-Babriel Peltirt. At the start of the French Revolution Charlotte was recruited as a spy and agent by Louise de Frotté for the counter-revolutionary royalists, from 1791 to 1794.

Known for her attempts to help the former royal escape from prison, she made many attempts to help Marie Antoinette, on one occasion visiting Marie in her prison cell dressed as a national guard. She also tried to free the former royal children from a temple. At one stage a child believed to be the Dauphin was smuggled out to Charlotte, but the child turned out to be mute.

A letter from Lady Jerningham from Lille in 1784 states:

A great many people have taken refuge here, to fly from their creditors in England: Among the rest a Norwich Family and a Mrs Atkins [*sic*] of Ketteringham. She was a player, a friend of Miss Younger. You may remember

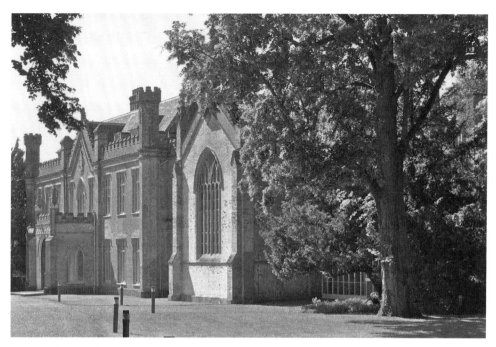

Ketteringham Hall.

to have heard of her and he was always a great simpleton or else he would not have married her.

Between November and December 1789, Monsieur Durez of Lille leased a house in his possession to an Englishwoman who went by the name Milady Charlotte. The house was situated at No. 337 Rue de Princesse. It was a few minutes away from the gates of the great military citadel that dominated Lille. The register for the poll tax for the seven parishes, 1778, declares,

> *Parish of St André Dec 1789 – Milady Charlotte, pensioner of*
> *France – No 337 Rue de Princesse (M. de Durez, owner)*
> Tax 12 livres
> For 1 servant 2 livres

Charlotte tried to follow the Dauphin after his exfiltration of the temple in Paris in 1794. She went in to the Gaillon in 1821 to see the false Dauphin, Mathurin Bruneau (Louis XVII) in jail there, but even with money she was not able to free him.

In 1834 she went to see Louis XVII, alias 'le Baron de Richemont', in jail at Ste Pélagie in Paris for the last time.

Edward died at Ketteringham Hall on 27 March 1794, and to continue to help the émigré problem Charlotte mortgaged Ketteringham Hall in 1799 and became involved in home politics, being part of the management team of John Wodehouse's unsuccessful campaign to be elected the member for Norfolk in 1806.

After the restoration of Louis XVIII in 1814, Charlotte petitioned for payments between £30,000 and £40,000 to cover all her expenditure, but the French government refused this. In 1824 she made over Ketteringham Hall to her sister-in-law, Mary Atkyns.

As the nineteenth century came to its end, the life of Mrs Atkyns came to be forgotten, except for in Mr O. Alger's book *English Men in the French Revolution* published in 1889 (she is mentioned on one page), but in 1896 Victoire Sardou, the celebrated French dramatist, produced his play *Pamela, Marchande de Frivolités* at the Vaudeville in Paris, which told the story of Charlotte Atkyns.

When the Prince of Wales was voted by Parliament into the Regency, due to his father's condition of madness, he celebrated the event with a party at his London home. Charlotte was among the 2,000 people invited to the grand fete and banquet given at Carlton House, Lower Regent Street, which cost £15,000.

Described by many as an eccentric not to be taken seriously, she lived for the remainder of her life in poverty after financially helping so many. She became known at the female Scarlet Pimpernel.

During the cold evening of 2 February 1836, Charlotte lay dying in her bed at No. 65 Rue de Lille with her loyal German maid, Victoire Ile. In her will Charlotte stated that she wished to be buried in the churchyard at Kettering, but this wish was not carried out. Her sister-in-law, Mary Atkyns, held the Kettering estate, but had died three months previously.

Charlotte died in Paris and is buried in an unknown grave. There is a memorial on the north wall of the nave of Ketteringham Church near her husband's family seat of Ketteringham Hall.

In the British feature film *A Tale of Two Cities*, a young lady says 'you won't get past me for I am an English woman'. Could this character have been based on Charlotte?

The WILL of MRS CHARLOTTE ATKYNS
January 6th 1835

I Charlotte Atkyns, give to Victoire Ile, my maid-servant, at present in my service, all effects of furniture, linen, wearing apparel and silver that I possess; and generally all objects which may be found in my room, in my house, or

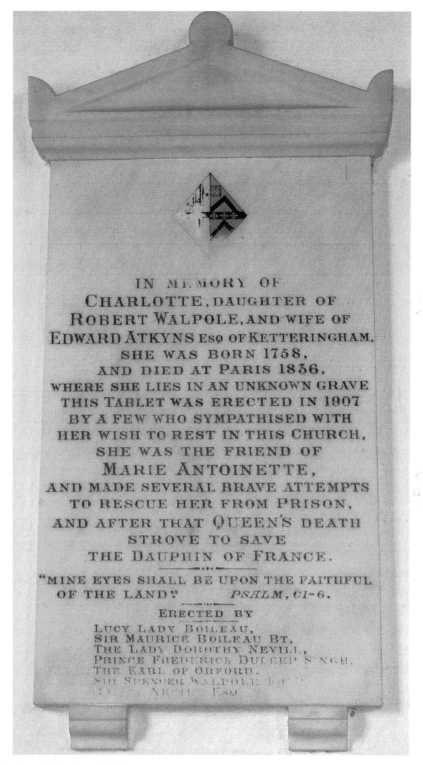

Ketteringham Church wall plaque.

lodging, at the date of my decease, whatever they may be; and also my carriage. I give moreover to the said Victoire Ile the sum of £120 sterling, which is due to me today from Nathaniel William Peach, of 13 Savile St London, and of Ketteringham in the County of Norfolk, or from his heirs, which shall be paid on demand to the said Victoire Ile, after my decease. I further give to Victoire Ile the sum of £1000 Stirling, which shall be paid to her with three months of my death.

I charge these gifts on the Norfolk property, which is at present in the hands of Nathanial W. Peach as a guarantee for all my debts, I having mortgaged the said property in favour of my sister-in-law, the late Mary Atkyns, for £1800 sterling, and in addition for an annuity of £500 sterling, payable quarterly each year; and as consequence belongs to me, I charge it with the payable of my lawful debts, and of my funeral expenses.

I desire that my body be taken to Kettering and interred in the family vault; and that my name and age be inscribed on a plain marble stone, near the monument of my late dear son. I have mentioned in another will the names of some friends from whom I beg acceptance of some souvenirs of my consideration and esteem. I give the box which I have left with Messrs Barnard & Co, Bankers, Cornhill, London, to Mr Nathaniel W. Peach. It contains some pieces of silver. I left it there, I think on Nov 10th 1832. I give the freehold of all my properties in Norfolk to Nathanial W. Peach for the payment of all charges and debts present and future. I give £100 sterling to my servant, Jean-Baptiste Erard, native of Switzerland, who has served me faithfully for five years, and whose conduct has always been regular. As to that of Victoire Ile, ever since she came into my service, it has been beyond all praise. The girl was not born to wait upon others; she belonged to a very respectable family of Munich. I appoint Nathaniel W. Peach my executor. I request that immediately after my death the Counsel for the British Embassy, Mr Okey (or whoever may be counsel at the time) may be sent for; and I desire him to be good enough to act for Nathaniel W. Peach here at Paris.

In the name of God, I sign the present testament.

[Nathanial W. Peach was a London Solicitor who was Charlotte's mother's nephew.]

A note in newspapers:

Mrs Charlotte Atkyns deceased.
If the next of kin (if any) of Charlotte Atkyns, formerly of Ketteringham, in the County of Norfolk, but late of the City of Paris, widow, deceased, will apply

to Mr William Jenkins, of No. 25 Coleshill-street, Pimlico, in the County of Middlesex, Gentlemen they may hear of something to their advantage.

A note among Winston's Theatrical Jottings at the Folger Library, dated 1790:

Mrs Atkins, late Miss Walpole of Drury Lane Theatre., is perhaps the most enterprising, entertaining female equestrian. This lady whose residence is at lisle in Flanders frequently rides for an airing ... to Calais which is seventy-four miles and returns the following day with the greatest ease.

Barnes, Josephine (1912–1999)

Josephine Barnes (Doctor Josephine Barnes or Dame Alice Josephine Mary Taylor Barnes, DBE) was born 18 August 1912 in Sheringham to Walter Wharton Barnes, a Methodist minister, and Alice Mary (*née* Ibbetson) who was a musician.

From Sheringham the family moved to Basingstoke, Exeter, Scarborough and then to Oxford where Josephine was educated at Oxford High School before going on to the University of Oxford to read natural sciences, followed

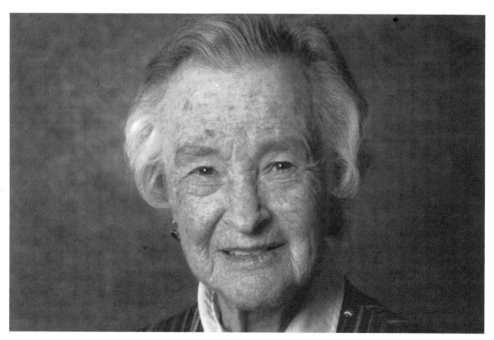

Dame Josephine Barnes.

by medicine at University College London. She became a leading obstetrician and gynaecologist and during the Second World War she met and married Lt Brian Warren. By 1954 she had become the first female consultant obstetrician and gynaecologist at Charing Cross Hospital.

In 1967 Josephine became involved in the public debate over the 1967 Abortion Act, and from 1979 to 1980 she was the first female president of the British Medical Association.

Josephine became a guardian at Westminster Abbey and a fellow of the Royal College of Physicians, the Royal College of Surgeons of England and the Royal College of Obstetricians and Gynaecologists.

Barwell, Louisa Mary (1800–1875)

Louisa Mary Barwell (*née* Bacon) was the daughter of Richard Mackenzie Bacon and his wife Jane Louisa (*née* Noverre). A musician and educational writer, Louisa was born in the parish of St Peter Mancroft in Norwich on 4 March 1800. By the time she was eighteen she was working with her father, editing the *Quarterly Musical Magazine and Review*.

After Louisa's marriage to Norwich wine merchant John Barwell, she devoted her time to the composition of educational works, and she also contributed to the *Quarterly Journal of Education*.

John shared Louisa's interests and they secured a scheme by which a charity day school in Norwich for girls was converted into an industrial training school, and they also formed friendships in Norwich's literary society.

Louisa's closest friend was Lady Noel Byron. Her publications of music were many and 'Childhood Hours' of 1851 was ordered by Queen Victoria to be used in the Royal nursery. 'Flora's Horticultural Fête' was chosen for the 1880 benefit of the Children's Infirmary, which was established at Norwich by her friend Jenny Lind.

Bedingfield, Frances (1616–1704)

Frances was the daughter of Francis and Katherine Fortescue Bedingfield and she was born in Norfolk in 1616. The family had remained Roman Catholic and she and her eleven sisters went into religious orders. Because of the Penal

Laws, Frances went to an order in Munich, of which she would later become the superior of the mother house.

It was on the orders of Queen Catherine of Braganza in 1699 that Frances was sent back to England to be the founder of school of the Institute in London. Frances then helped to set up a school for young women in St Martin's Lane and then in Hammersmith. To avoid persecution Frances wore a plain grey dress and used the alias of Mrs Long.

In 1677, Sir Thomas Gascoigne invited Frances to open the Bar Convent in York, which became the first convent to open in England after the Dissolution of the Monasteries; it was named after the neighbouring Micklegate Bar. The inspiration for the building came from the ideas of May Ward, who created the Congregation of Jesus and the Institute of the Blessed Virgin Mary. In 1696 the house was saved by a mob attack after the appearance of St Michael. Next was a boarding school for Catholic girls and in 1699 a free day school was set up. The convent school closed in 1985 and the Bar Convent is the oldest surviving convent in England.

Frances was arrested three times but her family name kept her from receiving far greater punishment. In 1694, along with her great-niece Mother Dorothy Pastor Bedingfield, she was taken to a magistrate before being taken to the Orse Bridge Gaol in York. The York community was outraged by this and the gaol was nearly destroyed.

Frances resigned in 1699 as Superior for her niece to take over, and she retired back to Munich and died on 4 May 1704.

A school called St Mary's, which was founded in 1885 in Ascot by Frances' successors, was named in honour of her.

Bendish, Bridget (1650–1726)

Bridget Bendish (*née* Ireton) was born in 1650 to General Henry Ireton and Bridget, who was Oliver Cromwell's eldest daughter. Born in Nottinghamshire, she was married to Thomas Bendish, a leading member of the Independent or Congregational Church of Yarmouth and went to live in Great Yarmouth where Thomas owned salt marshes and a salt works on Cobholme Island.

According to a contemporary sketch by Ipswich minister Samuel Say, 'She was a rigid calvimst of uncertain temper, with a strength of will and physical courage rarely paralleled.'

She championed her grandfather's reputation when travelling to London in a public coach when a fellow passenger spoke lightly of Cromwell. Not only did Bridget inveigh against the person, but on reaching London she snatched another passenger's sword from its sheath and challenged the slanderer to fight there and then.

Bridget was educated under the careful watch of her grandfather and he taught her never to divulge a secret; like Cromwell, she was known to have the strength of understanding.

Bridget and her husband were very much interested in politics, but compromised themselves often, as shown by the Rye House plot of 1683. In 1685 she tried to help her brother Henry, who was Lieutenant-Colonel of Dragoons and Captain of the horse to William III, escape from prison, charged as he was with suspicion of complicity. Henry was recaptured and sent to Newgate in London. Between the years 1688 to 1689 she released documents secretly recommending the recognition of William III.

During the reigns of Charles II and James II she became a member of the nonconformists and was a member of Dr John Owen's congregation in London. It was also said that Bridget was in the secret of the revolution, and to promote it she would visit shops in different parts of London under the pretence of cheapening silks and other articles – it was through this that Archbishop Tillotson introduced Bridget to Queen Mary and there was talk of a pension being awarded to her.

Another incident of Bridget doing battle for her grandfather took place when her aunt, Lady Fauconberg, and others said things to dishonour his memory. Bridget raised herself up, and with great spirit said, 'If I did not believe my grandmother to have been one of the most virtuous women in the world, I should conclude your ladyship to be a bastard, wondering how it could be possible that the daughter of the greatest and best man that ever lived could be so degenerate as not only to sit with patience to hear his memory so ill-treated, but to seem herself to assent to it.'

Thomas died in 1707 and left the businesses to Bridget, who was not good when it came to matters of money. She also squandered a bequest from her Lady Fauconberg, leading Bridget to see out her life on her own exertions.

Isaac Watts's poem 'Against Tears', addressed to Bridget in 1699, was written for her encouragement.

But tears, alas! are trifling things,
  They rather feed than heal our woe;
From trickling eyes now sorrow springs,
  As weeds in rainy seasons grow.

Thus weeping urges weeping on;
  In vain our miseries hope relief:
For one drop calls another down,
  Till we are drown'd in seas of grief.

Then let these useless streams be staid,
  Wear native courage in your face;
These vulgar things were never made
  Four souls of a superior race.

If 'tis rugged path you go,
  And thousand foes your steps surround,
Tread the thorns down, charge through the foe:
  The hardest fight is highest crown'd.

When widowed, Bridget was left with an income of £200 to £300 a year. She made many financial losses. One of her schemes was to attend the neighbouring fairs to buy and sell cattle, travelling in a single-horse chaise.

Bridget died in 1726 and is buried in St Nicholas's church, Great Yarmouth, near the grave of John Carter, Oliver Cromwell's former friend and host.

Bentley, Elizabeth (1767–1839)

Elizabeth was born in 1767 to Elizabeth Lawrence and Daniel Bentley in Norwich. The family were well educated and Elizabeth received home tuition. Elizabeth's father died in 1783 after suffering from a stroke in 1777.

Elizabeth started to write poetry in 1785 and her first collection, *Genuine Poetical Compositions*, was published in 1791 with 1,935 subscribers, including her peers Elizabeth Carter, Elizabeth Montague, William Cowper and Hester Chapone.

In a letter dated 23 July 1790 addressed to her patron and first editor, the Revd John Walker, she stated that her father taught her reading, spelling and writing but never gave her 'the least idea of Grammar'.

The poet William Cowper was so impressed with Elizabeth that he subscribed to her first volume of work, *Genuine Poetical Compositions, on Various Subjects*, and compared her verse with Mary Leapor's of forty years before. Other subscribers included members of parliament, clergymen, Cambridge dons, surgeons, attorneys and fellow writers.

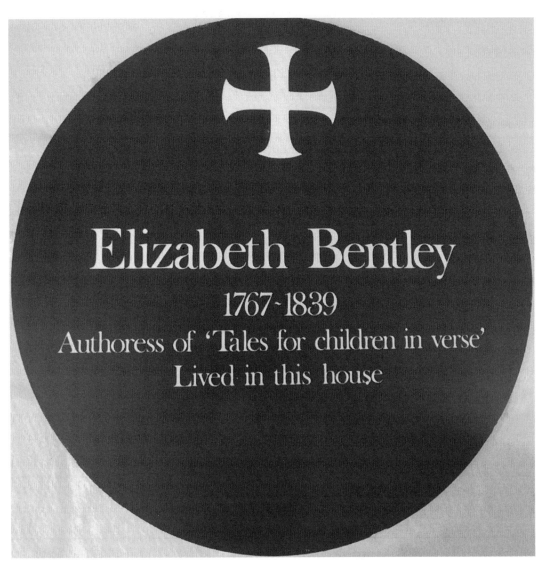

Elizabeth Bentley
1767-1839
Authoress of 'Tales for children in verse'
Lived in this house

Elizabeth Bentley plaque.

Elizabeth spent many years living at St Stephen's Square near the Norfolk and Norwich Hospital, of which she based the following poem:

See where yon spacious structure meets the eye!
    When, wing'd with zeal, intent on mortals' good,
Fair Charity, first offspring of the sky,
    Left her celestial realms for earth's abode.
Descending, here she fix'd her gracious seat;
    When Indigence the shaft of Pain receives,
Her hand conducts him to this blest retreat,
    Here soothes his anguish, and each woe relieves.

Here sage Professors of the healing art,
    Whose souls divine Benevolence inspires;
Their time employ, their wealth, their skill impart,
    Before whose eyes Death, with slow step, retires.
The halpless wretch to dire Disease a prey,
    From his untimely fate they kindly save;
With friendly hand each healing balm convey,
    And snatch the body from the gaping grave.
With equal care they teach the soul to trace
    Those regions for her future life design'd;
Expand the thoughts beyond earth's narrow space,
    And raise from dark Despair th' immortal mind.

Hail, sacred fabric! gen'rous mortals hail!
    By Charity inspir'd, these walls you fram'd;
Where'er her sway shall o'er the world prevail,
    Shall your unfading honours be proclaim'd.

Her poem to Admiral Lord Nelson, November 1800:

O! TRULY welcome to thy native land,
Thou first in glory mid her warlike band;
What shouts of triumph bade her shores resound,
When Victory's wreath thy valiant deeds had crown'd.
Our glowing hearts revere thy nobler mind,
Where beams each virtue of the brightest kind:

From pure Religion's source thy virtues flow,
Hence genuine Courage claims her dauntless brow;
The Christian hero's stedfast hopes repose
On Heav'n's firm rock—he fears no earthly foes.
Long blest with health, enjoy thy honours won!
While loyal Norfolk boasts her favourite son;
And O! may still th' Almighty's guardian care,
Preserve a life thy Country holds most dear.
May each brave warrior arm'd in Britain's cause,
Thus form his life by Wisdom's purest laws,
Thy great example ever in his view,
Then shall our land her impious foes subdue.

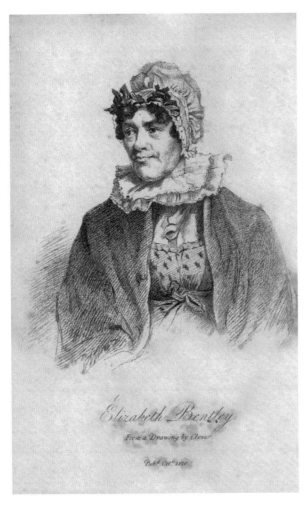

Elizabeth Bentley.

Very little was published after this, except *Battle of Trafalgar* in 1805 and *Poems* in 1821. The rest of her time was spent running a small boarding school, and except for the occasional poem in the *Norfolk Chronicle* (a small collection of verses for children, which was sold for a shilling), Elizabeth published nothing until *Poems; Being the Genuine Compositions of Elizabeth Bentley* in 1821, which was dedicated to John Wodehouse, Lord Lieutenant of Norfolk. Elizabeth died penniless at the Doughty's Hospital Almshouse in 1839 aged seventy-two, and is buried at St Stephen's, Norwich.

In her will Elizabeth left £10 to Seth William Stevenson from the printers who published her works, with the rest of her estate, less funeral expenses, going to Elizabeth Lawrence Whiting.

Elizabeth received the support of the Royal Literary Fund in 1799 and 1829.

Boadicea (d. AD 61)

There have been many great queens of England, but none so great as the formidable lady known as Queen Boudica or Boadicea. Queen Boadicea ruled the Iceni tribe of East Anglia with her husband King Prasutagus.

Trouble came to a head when King Prasutagus, who was working to win favour with the Romans, made the Roman Emperor Nero co-heir with his daughters to his kingdom and wealth. Prasutagus did this to keep his family safe from attacks on his household, but this was not fully achieved as the Roman governor of Britain, Suetonius Paulinus, had other ideas. After Prasutagus's death his household and all his lands were destroyed by Roman officers and their slaves. Boadicea was then publicly flogged and her daughters were raped by the Roman slaves.

After these vicious attacks the Iceni, Trinobantes and other tribes joined forces to fight against the Romans. The tribes first captured Camulodunum (Colchester), making the Imperial agent flee to Gaul. When the allies took Londinium (London) and Verulamium (St Albans), the settlements were sacked and burned. Even the local cemeteries were desecrated, along with statues that today can be seen in Colchester Museum.

Suetonius Paulinus withdrew and fled with his armies to the safety of the Roman military zone and, having decided to attack Boadicea, put together an army of 10,000 that were made up from the 14th Legion.

Tacitus, the Roman historian, gave a clear account of the final battle, which took place in the Midlands in AD 61.

Before the battle took place, Boadicea and her daughters drove around in her chariot to all the tribes for a last-minute talk, stating, 'Win the battle or perish: that is what I, a woman will do; you men can live on in slavery if that's what you want.'

To help the Romans, the Roman cavalry was released and Tacitus recorded that 80,000 Britons – men, women and children – were killed. The loss to the Romans was 400, with double that being injured.

Boadicea took her own life by poison rather than being taken prisoner; the site of her final battle is still unknown. Some claim it was at Battle Bridge Road, King's Cross, London, and that Boadicea is buried under a platform at King's Cross Station. Most historians state it to be in the West Midlands, with some claiming it to be in Leicestershire. Warwickshire has also been mentioned.

In 1902 a bronze statue of Boadicea by Thomas Thorneycroft was erected on the Thames embankment next to the Houses of Parliament.

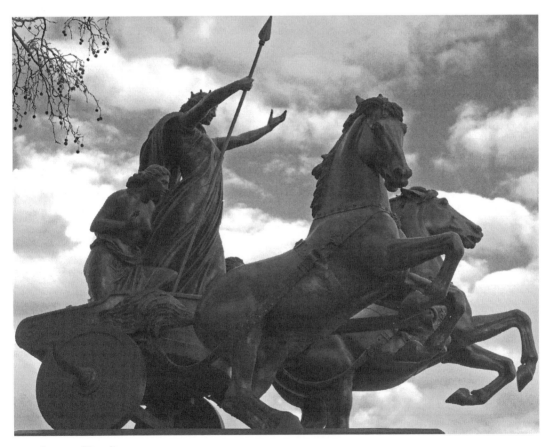

Statue of Boudicea.

Bohemia, Anne of (1366–1394)

Anne was born on 11 May 1366 and died on 7 June 1394. She became Queen of England after marrying King Richard II (she was his first wife). Anne was from the House of Luxembourg and she was the eldest daughter of Charles IV, Holy Roman Emperor and King of Bohemia, and Elizabeth of Pomerania. In 1383 Anne of Bohemia visited Norwich and at the Great Hospital a ceiling showing 252 black eagles was made in her honour, which represented the eagles of the Austrian Imperial Emblem.

Anne died of the plague in 1394, aged twenty-eight. Richard's grief was intense and, as some would say, destabilising, and he had Sheen Palace where Anne died destroyed. Anne was buried at Westminster near to Edward the Confessor's shrine.

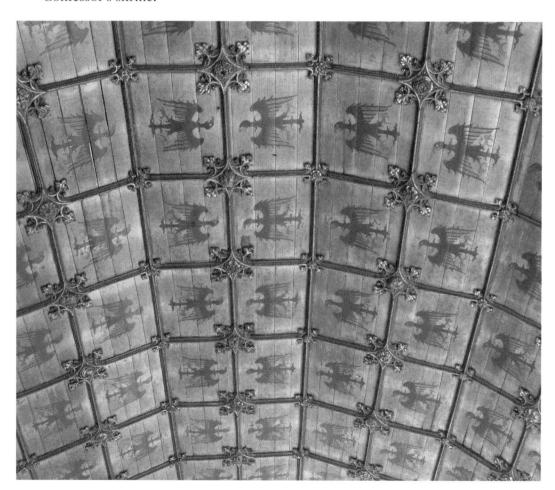

Anne of Bohemia Great Hospital ceiling.

Boleyn, Anne (1507–1536)

Anne Boleyn was Queen of England from 1533 to 1536, as the second wife of Henry VIII, and Marquess of Pembroke in her own right. Her father was Thomas Boleyn, 1st Earl of Wiltshire and her mother was Lady Elizabeth Howard.

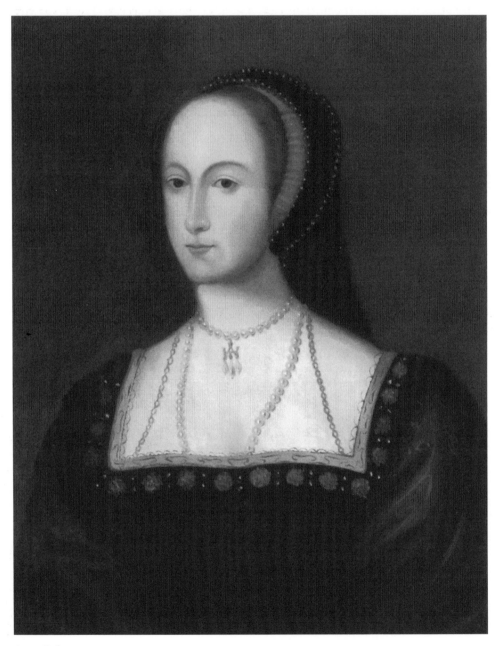

Anne Boleyn.

The family had their origins in the Norfolk village of Salle, and Anne's great-great-grandfather Geoffrey Boleyn found himself before the manorial court several times for trespassing and taking water from the manor without payment.

Not wanting his son, also named Geoffrey, to be poor, Geoffrey set him up as a hatter in London during the 1430s and he became successful and wealthy, joining the prestigious Mercer's Company in 1435. He served as Lord Mayor of London in 1457, and while married to his second wife Anne Hoo, the daughter of a baron, he purchased the manor of Blickling.

Anne may well be remembered for the role that she played in the English Reformation, but her family had connections with the twelfth-century Archbishop of Canterbury, Thomas Becket. Anne's great-grandfather, Thomas Butler, 7th Earl of Ormond, was buried in the church of St Thomas Acon in London, and it has been claimed that the church was built on the site of Becket's birthplace. The Butlers also claimed descent from another of Becket's sisters, who had married an Irish gentleman. The family also claimed a family heirloom, a white ivory horn garnished with gold, that was claimed to have been the cup from which Becket drank. The 7th Earl gave the white ivory horn to his grandson, Sir Thomas Boleyn, who went on to pass it to his own male heirs.

Anne was born at Blickling Hall and educated in France. She came back to England in 1522 to marry her Irish cousin James Butler, 9th Earl of Ormond. This did not take place and instead she became a maid of honour to Catherine

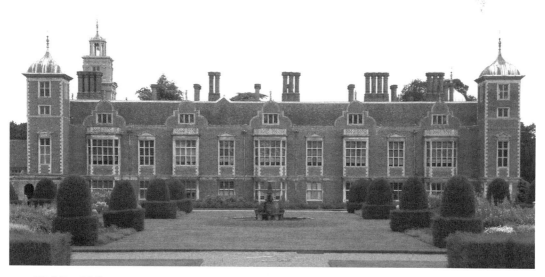

Blickling Hall.

of Aragon. Both her father, Sir Thomas, and James's father, Piers, claimed the earldom of Ormond, which was once owned by her great-grandfather. An agreement was made in 1528 when Sir Thomas became Earl of Ormond and Piers Butler became Earl of Ossory.

The first recorded appearance of Anne at court was on 1 March 1522 at a masque. Henry Percy, heir to the earldom of Northumberland, took an interest in Anne, and this was noticed at court by William Cavendish, a friend of Percy's, but he was also in the services of Cardinal Wolsey. Anne and Percy fell in love and even planned to marry. When the relationship was discovered by Wolsey, he berated Percy, stating that he was marrying beneath himself, and for a short time Anne was banished from court.

While it is known by many that Anne's sister Mary was Henry VIII's mistress, a rumour went around court that their mother, Elizabeth Howard, also shared a bed with the king. By 1533 the wife of a London Goldsmith, Elizabeth Amadas, stated publicly that Thomas Boleyn 'was bawd both to his wife and his two daughters', and Sir George Throckmorton told the king to his face that 'it is thought you have meddled both with the mother and sister'.

Anne's mother was also the first cousin of Jane Seymour's mother, Margery Wentworth, and the cousins were raised together at Sheriff Hutton Castle in Yorkshire under the protection of Elizabeth's mother Elizabeth Tylney, Countess of Surrey, who was also half-sister to Margery's mother.

The following is from Cranmer's own account contained in a letter from him to Mr Hawkyns, English Ambassador at the court of Emperor Charles V:

Queen Anne Boleyn: Her Coronation
Whitsunday 1 June, 1533

… The Thursday next before the Feast of Pentecost, the King and Queen being at Greenwich, all the crafts of London thereunto well appointed, in several barges decked after the most gorgeous and sumptuous manner, with divers pageants thereunto belonging, repaired and waited all together upon the Mayor of London; and so well furnished, came all unto Greenwich, where they tarried and waited for the Queen's coming to her barge; which so done, they brought her unto the tower, trumpets, shawms and other divers instruments playing and making great melody, which, as is reported, was as comely done as never was like in any time nigh to our remembrance. And so her grace came to the Tower on Thursday at night, about five of the clock, where also was such a peal of guns hath not been heard the like a great while before. And the same night, and Friday all day, the King and Queen tarried there; and on Friday at night the King's grace made eighteen Knights of the Bath, whose creation was not only so strange to hear of, as also their garments stranger to behold or look upon; which said Knights, the next day, which was Saturday, rode before the Queen's grace throughout the City of London towards Westminster Palace, over and besides the most part of the nobles of the realm, which like accompanied her grace throughout the said City, she sitting in her hair [i.e. her hair flowing down] upon a horse litter, richly apparelled, and four Knights of the five ports bearing a canopy over her head and after her came four rich chariots, one of them empty, and three other furnished with divers ancient old ladies; and after them came a great train of other ladies and gentlewomen; which said progress, from the beginning to the ending, extended half a mile in length by estimation or thereabout. To whom also, as she came along, the City, where shewn many costly pageants, with divers other encomiums spoken of children to her; wine also running at certain conduits plenteously. And so proceeding throughout the streets, passed further unto Westminster Hall, where was a certain banquet prepared for her, which done, she was conveyed out of the back side of the palace into a barge, and so unto York Place where the King's grace was before her coming, for this you must ever presuppose that his grace came always before her secretly in a barge as well from Greenwich to the Tower as from the Tower to York Place.

The Sunday was the coronation, which also was of such a manner.

In the morning there assembled with me at Westminster Church the Bishop of York, the Bishop of London, the Bishop of Winchester, the Bishop of Lincoln, the Bishop of Bath and the Bishop of St Asaph, the Abbot of Westminster with ten or eleven more Abbots, which all revestred ourselves in our pontificalibus, and, so furnished, with our crosses and croziers, proceeded out of the Abbey in a procession into Westminster Hall, where we received the Queen apparelled in a robe of purple velvet, and all the ladies and gentlewomen in robes and gowns of scarlet according to the manner used before in such business; and so her grace sustained of each side with two Bishops, the Bishop of London and the Bishop of Winchester, came forth in procession unto the Church of Westminster, she in her hair, my Lord of Suffolk bearing before her the crown, and two other Lords bearing also before her a sceptre and a white rod, and so entered up into the high altar, where divers ceremonies used about her, I did set the crown on her head, and then was sung Te Deum. And after that was sung a solemn mass, all which while her grace sat crowned upon a scaffold which was made between the high altar and choir in Westminster Church; which mass and ceremonies done and finished, all the assembly of noblemen brought her into Westminster Hall again, where was kept a great solemn feast all that day; the good order thereof were too long to write at this time to you.

But now sir, you may not imagine that this coronation was before her marriage, for she was married much about St Paul's day last, as the condition thereof doth well appear by reason she is now somewhat big with child. Notwithstanding it hath been reported throughout a great part of the realm that I married her, which was plainly false, for I myself knew not thereof a fortnight after it was done. And many other things be reported of me, which be more lies and tales ....

While married to the King, Anne was aware of the burgeoning relationship between her husband and her maid, Jane Seymour. In the early months of 1536 Henry gave Jane his picture, which she wore around her neck. On seeing this, Anne saw red and ripped the chain from Jane, hurting her own hand during the process. Jane Dormer, who served under Princess Mary, stated that there were many fights between Anne and Jane.

A legend stated that Ann had a sixth finger and a large mole or goiter on her neck, but the moles could have been beauty marks.

A musician in Anne's household named Mark Smeaton was arrested on 30 April 1536, and after he was interrogated a series of arrests took place. Anne was taken to the Tower of London on 2 May accused of adultery and incest. While at the Tower Anne made knowledge of her conversations with Mark Smeaton and Henry Norris. The conversations were noted by the lieutenant of the Tower and passed on to the King. Because Sir Francis Weston once professed his love for Anne, he too was arrested and executed; four others were also executed on 17 May 1536. Anne was executed two days later and buried in the chapel of St Peter ad Vincula at the Tower of London. Seventeen love letters from Henry to Anne are preserved in the Vatican Library.

Anne's heart was reputedly discovered in 1836 in the south wall of the church of Elveden Park, Thetford, and reburied near her organs.

When Elizabeth I became Queen, her mother Anne was venerated as a martyr and heroine of the English Reformation.

Brightwell, Cecilia Lucy (1811–1875)

Cecilia was born at Thorpe in Norwich on 27 February 1811, the eldest child of Thomas Brightwell and his first wife, Mary Snell. Thomas was a nonconformist solicitor and mayor of Norwich, a microscopist and writer to scientific journals, going on to discover *Asplanchna brightwellii*, a species of rotifer. Her uncle, Simon Wilkin, edited the works of Sir Thomas Browne.

Cecilia was an Italian scholar and brilliant etcher, and her philanthropic spirit was shown in her contribution of the sum of £180 for the Brightwell lifeboat which was placed on the Norfolk coast at Blakeney.

Her writings, which were published by the Religious Tract Society, were mainly biographical and for the young. Her most important work was her first work, the *Life of Amelia Opie*.

Cecilia suffered with cataract problems, as did her father, and she died at Norwich on 17 April 1875. She is buried at the Rosary Cemetery beside her father.

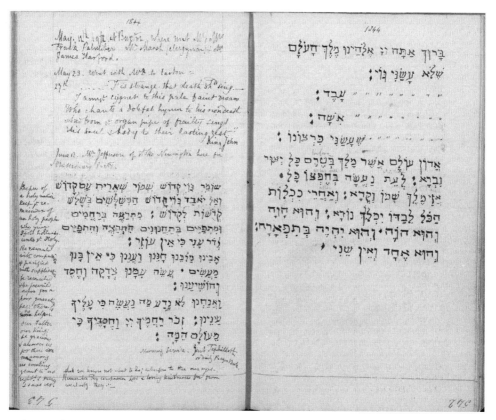

Religious diary of Cecilia Lucy Brightwell.

Brunton, Elizabeth (1799–1860)

Elizabeth, born in Norwich on 21 January 1799, was an actress who appeared under the names Miss Brunton, Elizabeth Brunton, Elizabeth Yates, and Mrs Yates. Her grandfather, John Brunton, acted at Covent Garden in 1774, and her father, John Brunton, also appeared at Covent Garden in 1800. Elizabeth was the niece of Louisa, Countess of Craven.

She made her debut in 1815 at her father's theatre at Lynn and she enjoyed many different roles, playing at theatres in Worcester, Shrewsbury and Leicester. Elizabeth's London debut took place at Covent Garden in 1817 when she took the role of Letitia Hardy and of Rosalind in *As You like It*, but her father believed her talents lay in comedy.

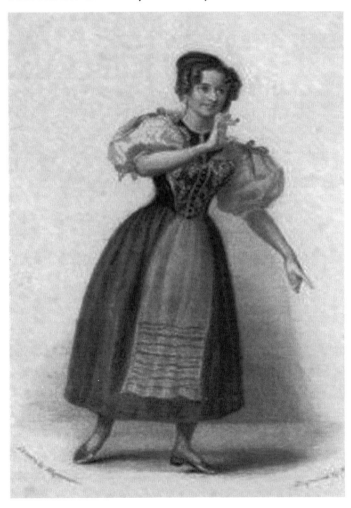

Elizabeth Yates.

Two years later in Edinburgh, Elizabeth reprised her role as Letitia Hardy, and back at Covent Garden she portrayed Lady Teazle in *The Clandestine Marriage*.

Elizabeth later joined her father at the West London Theatre, taking on roles in many plays including *She Stoops to Conquer* and *Three Weeks after Marriage*.

In her final season at Covent Garden she played Miss Prue in *Love for Love*, Sophia in *The Road to Ruin*, Dorinda in *Dryden's Tempest*, Elvira in *Love Makes a Man* and Clotilde de Biron in Thomas Morton's *Henri Quatre*.

She married fellow actor Frederick Henry Yates in November 1823 and appeared with him at Cheltenham. Henry died in June 1842, and Elizabeth was a manager for one year at the Adelphi Theatre. *The Times* described her as one of the most celebrated and highly esteemed actresses of domestic drama.

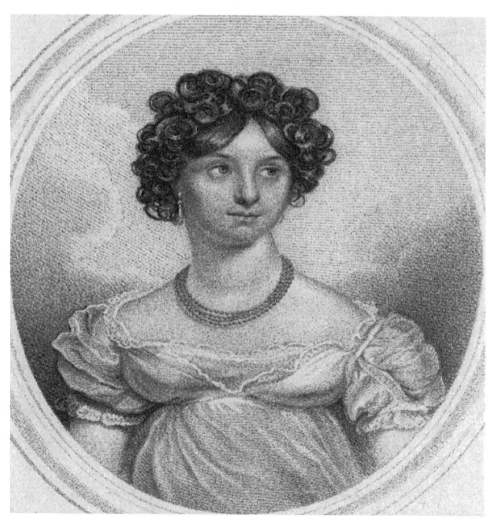

Mrs Brunton.

Bryden, Beryl Audrey (1920 –1998)

Beryl Audrey Bryden was born on 11 May 1920, at Rowington Road, Norwich, the only child of Amos and Elsie Bryden. She was educated at Norwich High School. By the time Beryl reached her teens she had fallen in love with Jazz music and she joined the local branch of the National Rhythm Club movement when she was seventeen, going on to establish a Nat Gonella fan club and becoming the secretary of the Norwich branch by 1941. Beryl also became friends with Black Anna Hannant, who was the landlady at the Jolly Butchers pub in Ber Street, Norwich.

On an early visit to London she heard black musicians were playing at the Jigs Club in Soho and it changed the course of her life.

Aged twenty-two, Beryl moved to Cambridge to run the city's Rhythm Club and began singing mainly Billie Holiday songs. By the time the Second World War ended, she had moved to London in her desire to be a big player in the jazz scene. Singing semi-professionally, she met with and started singing with Humphrey Lyttleton, Clinton Maxwell, George Webb, Cy Laurie, Mick Mulligan, George Melly and John Haim's Jelly Roll Kings, recording her debut in 1948 with trumpeter Freddy Randall. Playing with a metal washboard, she sang many songs by Bessie Smith. She also played at London Jazz venues such as the Cook's Ferret Inn, Walthamstow. When the Musicians Union ban was lifted she became friends with American musicians such as Buck Clayton, Louis Armstrong and Bud Freeman.

By 1949, Beryl formed 'Beryl's Back-Room Boys' and went on to broadcast regularly before she joined trumpeter Mike Daniels as the compère and singer at his Delta Jazz Club in Soho. It was while at this club in 1952 that she was introduced to French clarinettist Maxime Saury, who asked her to sing with his band at the Vieux Colombier in Paris, and this became her first professional engagement.

It was in Paris that she met American trumpeter Bill Coleman, singer Billie Holiday and Lou Williams, the pianist who Beryl recorded with.

Jazz established many fans in the 1950s. Beryl sang and recorded with the trombonist Chris Barber and she also played washboard with his singer, Lonnie Donegan. Their 1956 record 'Rock Island Line' went on to sell two million copies and entered the charts both here in England and the United States; Ella Fitzgerald claimed her as 'Britain's queen of the blues'.

In 1961, during the festival of Juan-les-Pins, Beryl appeared with Count Basie and the vocal group Lambert, Hendricks and Ross and Ray Charles.

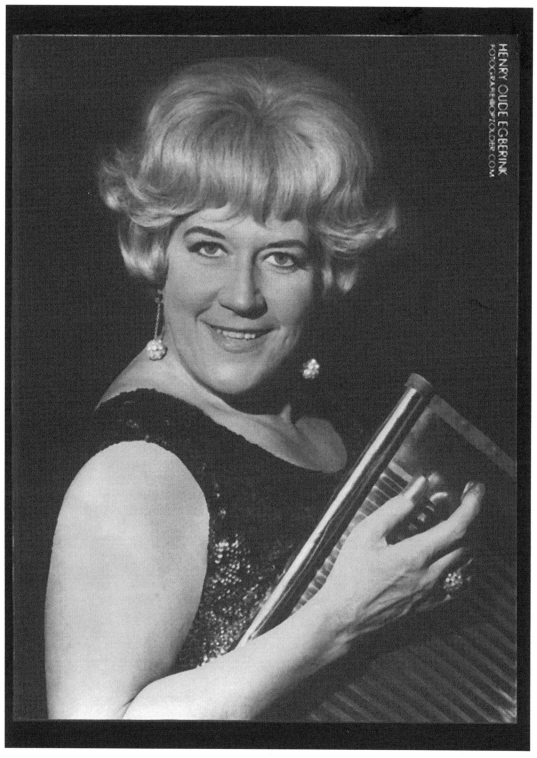

Beryl Bryden.

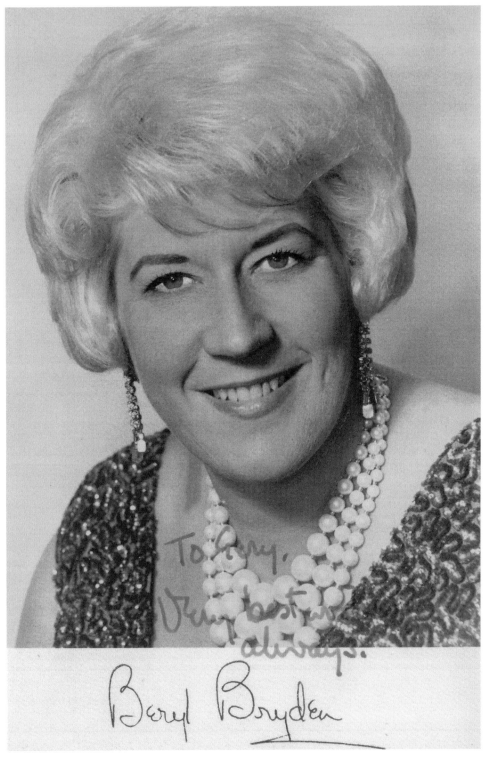

Beryl Bryden autograph.

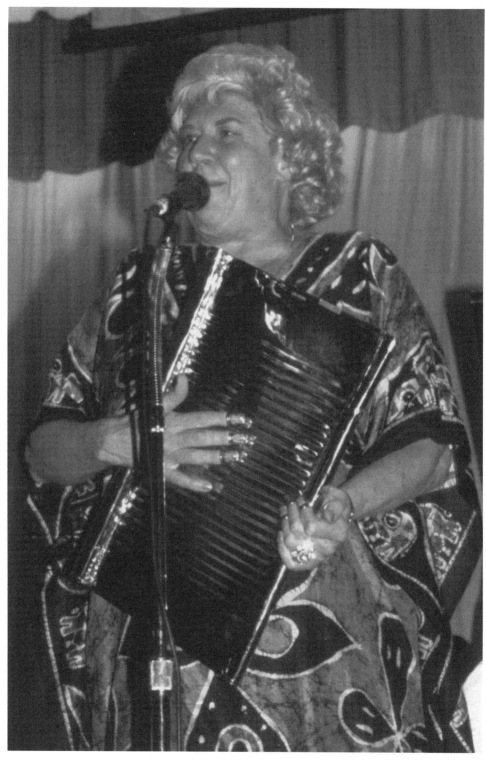

Beryl Bryden.

In the 1970s Beryl became the only British female jazz musician to be awarded the Freedom of the City of New Orleans.

Well known for her singing, Beryl was also known for her flamboyant gowns and sculptured blonde wigs, as well as her star-spangled washboard. While travelling with work she took up hobbies as diverse as photography and deep sea diving. She lived for many years in Gloucester Terrace, Paddington.

Beryl continued playing well into the 1990s with the Metropolitan Jazz Band, Digby Fairweather, Nat Gonella and her own Blue Boys. Her last recording was in 1998 with Nat Gonella.

Beryl died from cancer on 14 July 1998 at St Mary's Hospital, Paddington.

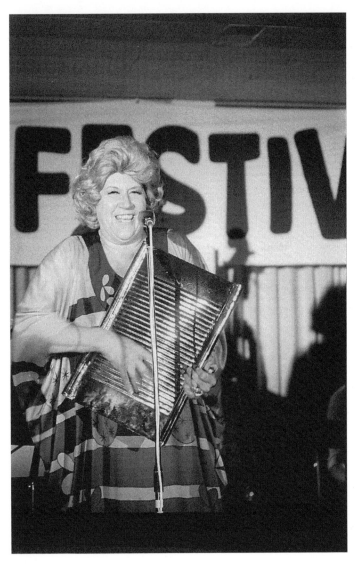

Beryl Bryden performing at a festival.

Burney, Fanny (1752–1840)

After her marriage, Fanny was known as Madame D'Arblay, novelist, diarist and playwright. She was born in Lynn Regis (now King's Lynn) to music historian Dr Charles Burney and Esther Sleepe Burney, and was a successful businesswoman who, along with her mother and sister, operated a number of fashionable London fan shops.

In 1784 a budding romance with clergyman George Owen Cambridge had come to an end, and at the age of thirty-three she remained unmarried. Through her acquaintance with Mary Delaney, Frances was introduced to the royal family.

Aged forty-two she married French exile General Alexandre D'Arblay and had a son called Alexander. She later settled in Bath.

Frances wrote four novels, eight plays, one biography, twenty-four journals and numerous letters. Her first novel, *Evelina*, was written anonymously in 1778. When the public found out that she was the author she was given overnight fame due to the comic strength it featured; all of her books satirised the English aristocrats. Her diaries, published posthumously in 1841, showed an amazing portrait of what life was like during the eighteenth century.

Burney's diaries are often cited in the modern Oxford English Dictionary, one particularly apt example being her coinage of the word 'journalist'.

Fanny's counted among her fans Dr Samuel Johnson, Edmund Burke, Hester Thrale and David Garrick. When her comedy novels were no longer enjoyed by her public, she took to writing tragedies.

Fanny's mother was a woman of great warmth and intelligence, the daughter of Dubois, a French refugee who died when Fanny was ten years old. Her father Charles was a musician and a writer of letters, who went on to marry Elizabeth Allen from King's Lynn. Charles's children from his first marriage did not get on with Elizabeth or her children.

Fanny's novels were enjoyed by arts patron Hester Thrale, and it was at his house in Streatham in London where she was first introduced to Doctor Johnson.

In her book *Cecilia*, the sentence, 'The whole of this unfortunate business ... has been the result of pride and prejudice', gave the novelist Jane Austen the title for one of her most famous books.

During the year 1775 Thomas Barlow asked Fanny to marry him after only meeting once, and she tells of the short courtship in one of her journals. In 1785 Mary Granville Delany, a woman involved in theatrical and royal

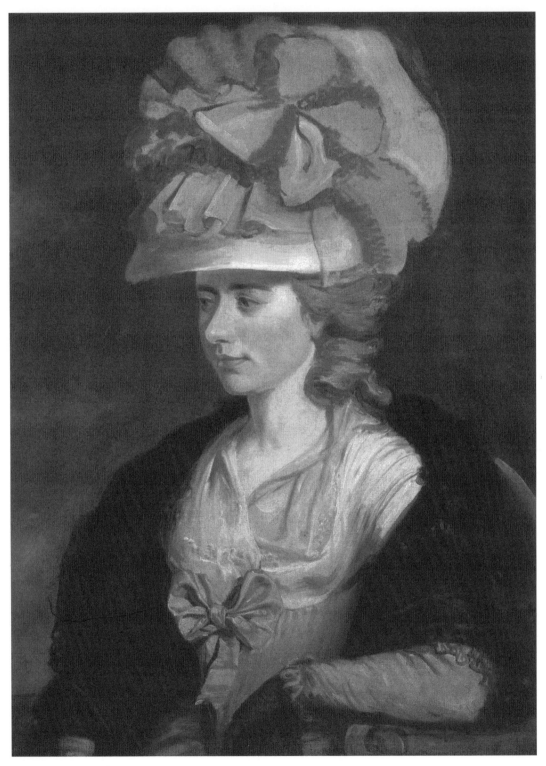

Young Fanny Burney.

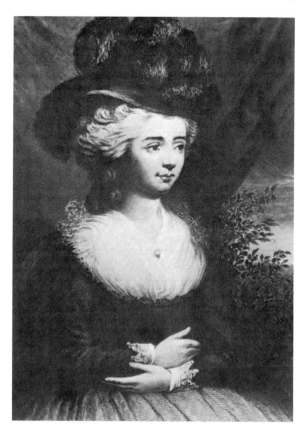

Fanny Burney.

circles, introduced Fanny to King George III and Queen Charlotte, and she was offered the position of Keeper of the Robes, which gave her a salary of £200 a year. Fanny continued to write her journals while at court. She also wrote to her recently married sister Susan, saying, 'I am now fitting out as you were, and all the maids and workers suppose I am going to be married.'

From 1790 to 1791 Frances wrote the tragedies *Hubert de Vere*, *The Siege of Pervensey*, *Elberta and Edwy* and *Elgiva*, which closed after one performance; all were blank verse tragedies.

When released from court, Frances spent much of her time in the early 1790s visiting her sister Susan Phillips at her home in Mickleham, Surrey.

By 1791 Frances was meeting up with Constitutionalists – French exiles – who fled to England to live at Juniper Hall, Mickleham. She became friendly with General Alexandre D'Arblay, an artillery officer who had been adjutant-general to the French Revolution leader Lafayette. Alexandre taught Frances to speak French and placed her in touch with the French writer Germaine de Staël.

Plaque.

Fanny and Alexandre were married on 28 July 1793. Her father was against the union because of Alexandre living in poverty and because of him being a Catholic. A year later their son Alexander was born and the family was saved from the poverty they found themselves in by the publication of the novel *Camilla*. Frances made £1,000 from the sale, followed by a further £1,000 for selling the copyright; they built Camilla Cottage in Westhumble with the money.

Frances went on to write three comedies which were not published while she was alive. During 1801 Alexandre was offered work in France with the government of Napoleon Bonaparte, and Frances and child followed. As the war between France and England took place, the family stayed there for ten years with the support of her family.

From 1785 to 1788
MRS MARY DELANY
(1700-1788)
Artist and friend of Royalty
lived here in a house
provided by
KING GEORGE III.

A frequent visitor was
the novelist and diarist

FANNY BURNEY
(1752-1840)
while engaged as
Keeper of the Robes to
QUEEN CHARLOTTE.

Plaque.

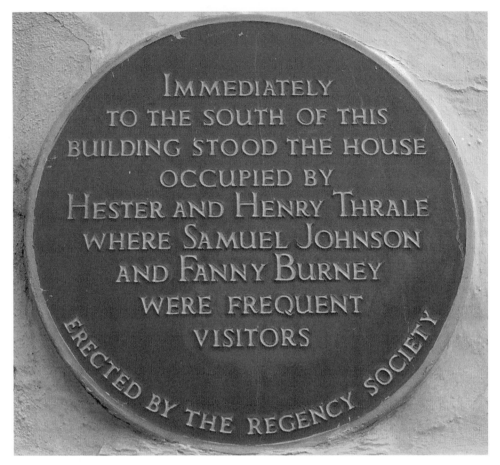

IMMEDIATELY
TO THE SOUTH OF THIS
BUILDING STOOD THE HOUSE
OCCUPIED BY
HESTER AND HENRY THRALE
WHERE SAMUEL JOHNSON
AND FANNY BURNEY
WERE FREQUENT
VISITORS
ERECTED BY THE REGENCY SOCIETY

Plaque.

In 1801 Frances developed breast pains, which her husband believed to be breast cancer, and through her royal connections she was attended to by the leading physicians of the day. On 30 September 1811 Frances underwent a mastectomy performed by Dr Larrey, M Dubois, Dr Moreau, Dr Aumont, Dr Ribe and pupils of Dr Larrey and M Dubois, who held the position of obstetrician to the Empress Marie Louise, Duchess of Parma.

Frances's experience was written down and sent to her sister Esther, and as of today it remains a compelling account of an early mastectomy. Frances, in 1812, returned to England to visit her father and to avoid the conscription into the French Army of Alexander. Her father died in 1814. Frances produced a journal from 1818 to 1832 called the Waterloo Journal. The year 1815 saw Napoleon escape from Alba, and Alexandre D'Arblay was promoted to lieutenant-general. He died of cancer in 1818.

Frances's fourth novel, *The Wanderer*, made her £1,500 and she moved to London to be with her son who was at Christ's College. This would be Frances's final novel. Set during the early 1790s against the backdrop of the French Revolution, this work was perhaps more political and yet was criticised by the British periodical press for its lack of engagement with politics, being compared unfavourably with Burney's earlier works.

In 1832 she published in three volumes the memoirs of Doctor Burney, her father, in which Frances recalls her educational backwardness among a family of precocious children, writing that 'at eight years of age she was ignorant of the letters of the alphabet', but that 'at ten, she began scribbling, almost incessantly, little words of invention; but always in private'. Just as Frances's 'scribbling' seems to have begun around the time of her mother's death, her writing seems to take on symbolic significance around the time of her father's remarriage, as Burney recalls, on her fifteenth birthday, making a bonfire of 'her whole stock of prose goods and chattels' with the sincere intention to extinguish forever in their ashes her scribbling propensity.

Alexander died in 1837 and Frances died 6 January 1840. She was buried with her husband and son in Walcot cemetery in Bath. A blue plaque was placed on her residence at No. 11 Bolton Street, Mayfair, London.

Cavell, Edith (1865–1915)

Edith Louisa Cavell was born on 4 December 1865 and executed on 12 October 1915. She was a renowned nurse, who saved the lives of soldiers on both sides during the First World War and helped Allied soldiers escape German-occupied Belgium. She was arrested, court-martialled, found guilty of treason and sentenced to death.

Edith was born to Louisa Sophia and Frederick Cavell in the village of Swardeston, where her father was the vicar. Edith was baptised at St Mary's church, Swardeston and it was here that she later worshipped. Both her parents are buried here, very close to the gate that linked their home and the churchyard.

In 1888 Edith became a governess at Keswick Hall, looking after the three children of the Gurney family. At the age of thirty she trained as a nurse at the London Hospital under the guidance of Matron Eva Luckes and later moved about many hospitals in the London area.

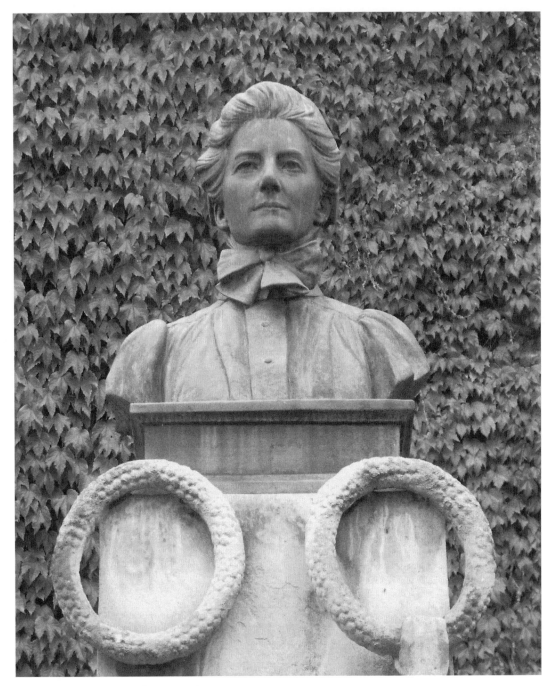

Edith Cavell Norwich memorial.

In 1907 Dr Antoine Depage recruited Edith to be the matron of the nursing school L'École Belge d'Infirmières Diplômées situated on the Rue de la Culture, Ixelles, in Brussels. By 1910 Edith used her professionalism to produce the journal '*L'infirmière*'. By 1911, Edith was a training nurse for three hospitals and thirteen kindergartens in Belgium.

She was back in Norfolk at the family home when the First World War broke out, and when she returned to Belgium the clinic and hospitals that she was associated with had been taken over by the Red Cross.

At the start of the war, and the German occupation of Brussels, Edith started to shelter British soldiers by funnelling them out of the country to the Netherlands, which was neutral. British soldiers and Belgian and French civilians were placed in secret houses and were provided with false papers by Prince Reginald de Croy at Bellignies near Mons. By doing this, it placed Edith in violation of German military law. Edith also became very vocal and the German authorities became aware of her. She was arrested on 3 August 1915 and charged with harbouring Allied soldiers. Held at Saint-Gilles prison for ten weeks, she soon realised that she had been betrayed by Gaston Quien, who would later be convicted by a court in France as having been a collaborator.

Edith admitted conveying sixty soldiers, fifteen French soldiers and up to 100 French and Belgians. Paragraph 58 of the German Military Code read, 'Will be sentenced to death for treason any person who, with the intention of helping the hostile Power, or of causing harm to the German or allied troops, is guilty of one of the crimes of paragraph 90 of the German Penal Code.'

The government in Britain were not able to help and Sir Horace Rowland of the Foreign Office said, 'I am afraid that it is likely to go hard with Miss Cavell; I am afraid we are powerless.' The Under-Secretary for Foreign Affairs, Lord Robert Cecil, stated, 'Any representation by us will do her more harm than good.'

Even though the United States had not joined the war, the First Secretary of the US legation at Brussels, Hugh S. Gibson, said to the Germans that if the execution of Edith went ahead it would further harm Germany's damaged reputation.

The German civil governor, Baron von der Lancken, stated that Edith should be pardoned because she helped so many German soldiers and had been so honest, but General von Sauberzweig, military governor of Brussels, said that in the interests of the state the death penalty against Baucq and Cavell should be immediate as this would stop other countries considering clemency.

Defended by Sadi Kirschen, twenty-seven were put on trial, and five, including Louise Thuliez, Séverin, and Countess Jeanne de Belleville, along with Edith and Baucq, were sentenced to death; only Edith and Baucq were executed.

On the evening of the execution Edith was in discussion with Revd Stirling Gahan who gave her Holy Communion. She stated, 'Patriotism is not enough. I must have no hatred or bitterness towards anyone.' The final words were given to the German Lutheran prison chaplain Paul Le Seur: 'Ask Father Gahan to tell my loved ones later on that my soul, as I believe, is safe, and that I am glad to die for my country.' Edith also stated that she faced death with calm courage.

After execution, Belgian ladies immediately buried her body next to Saint-Gilles prison. When the war was over the body was taken back to Britain and a memorial service was held. A state funeral took place in Westminster Abbey and then she was transferred to Norwich Cathedral, within the old monks' burial ground known as 'Life's Green'. It was the wishes of her family for her to be buried here rather than at Westminster Abbey. A graveside service is still held each year on 21 October.

At Erpingham Gate a statue of Edith by Henry Pegram was unveiled by Queen Alexandra on 12 October 1918. It was originally placed in the middle of the road opposite the Maids Head Hotel, which was once occupied by the Cavell Rest Home for Nurses.

The railway carriage that conveyed her remains from Dover to London is kept as a memorial on the Kent and East Sussex Railway. In late 2015, the railway carriage was being held outside the Forum in Norwich but has since returned to Bodiam railway station.

To commemorate the centenary in 2015, Edith's grave was to be restored. Concerts marked the event in Holy Trinity Pro-Cathedral, Brussels, and in Norwich on 19 October. They featured performances of the new Cavell Mass by David Mitchell, along with Haydn's Missa in angustiis. Edith Cavell is also featured on a £2 coin.

As this book was being completed, ex-MI5 chief Stella Rimington stated that Edith was spying on the Germans. The Germans always claimed this, although the British Government at the time vehemently denied it. A new radio show, broadcast just before the centenary, stated how Ms Rimington found evidence in military archives in Belgium claiming that Edith was operating a two-tier espionage system. Documents also found linked Edith to Secret Service Bureau agent Dr Tollemache Bull.

The work that Edith started is still in existence today, under the Cavell Nurse's Trust.

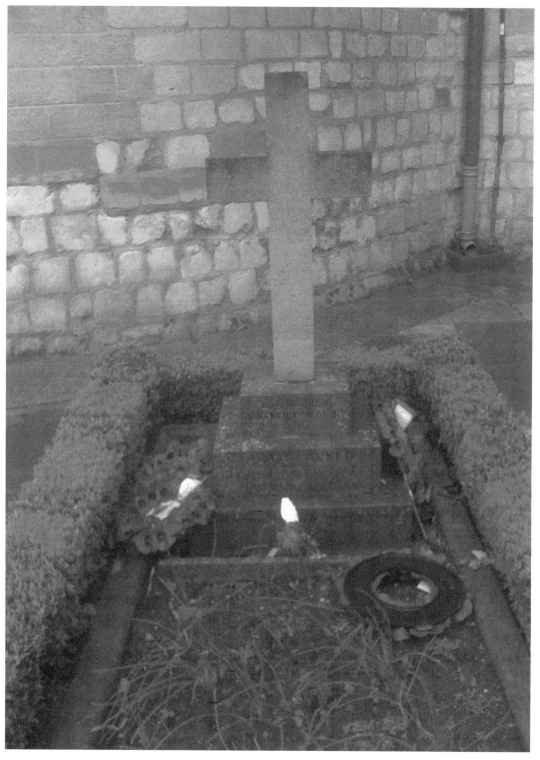

Edith Cavell's grave.

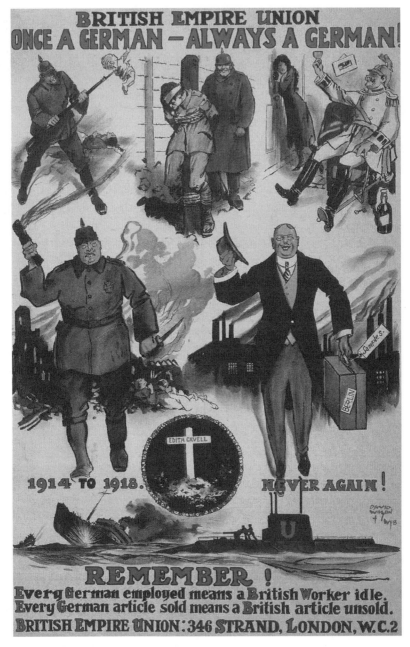

First World War poster.

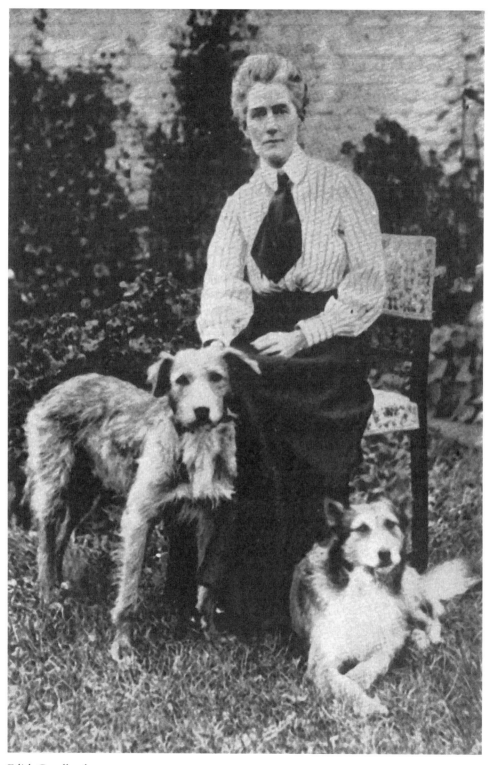

Edith Cavell at home.

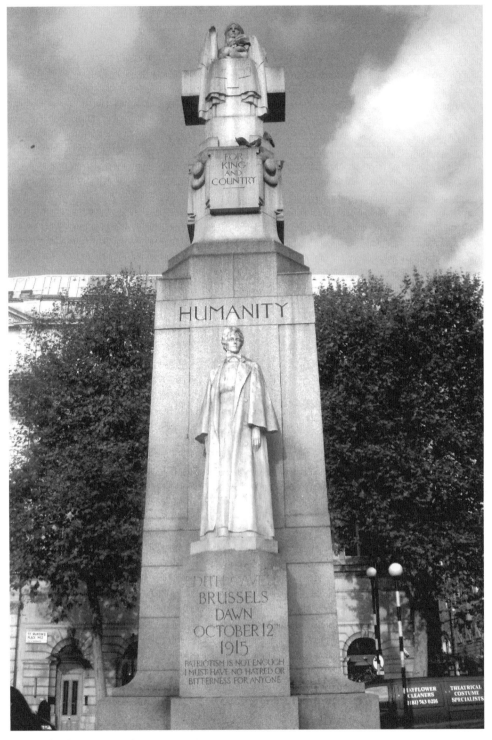

Edith Cavell statue, London.

Chapman, Mary (1647–1724)

Mary Chapman was born on 24 March 1647, the daughter of Alderman John Mann, said to be the richest man in Norwich, and Dorothy Fountaine. She married the rector of Thorpe, Samuel Chapman, on 10 May 1682; he died in 1700. The couple had no children. Both decided to establish a building of 'poor lunatics, and not for natural born fools or idiots'.

On 12 December 1712 the city committee granted a lease to four men who were acting as trustees on behalf of Mary. A piece of ground was granted on a peppercorn rent for 1,000 years. John Morse, one of the trustees, built the house, which was completed in 1713.

Mary died in 1724, and in her will she changed the private institution into an independent public trust that would be managed by a committee and would be regulated by certain instructions.

Originally the hospital opened in 1713 and became the first purpose-built asylum in the country, the other being the Bethlehem Hospital in London. The site in Committee Street was later changed to Bethel Street.

At a cost of £314 2s 6d, the hospital was built by Richard Starling and Edward Freeman. In 1899, the great architect of Norwich, Edward Boardman, remodelled the front. An inscription on the foundation stone reads:

> This house was built for the benefit of the distrest Lunaticks Ano Dom. 1713 and is not to be alienated or employed to any other use or purpose whatsoever. Tis also requir'd that the Master, who shall be choosen from time to time, be a Man that lives in the Fear of God and sets up true protestant Religion in his Family and will have a due Regard as well to souls as bodies are those under his care.

All of the patients were protected against exploitation, fire, self-injury, assault, excessive physical restraint and escape. At one there were twenty-five residents and the inventory had five pairs of handcuffs, ten padlocks and two chains and staples. In 1758 waistcoats for disorderly lunatics were used.

When the NHS came in to service, the Bethel became part of Hellesdon Hospital. In 1962 it became the oldest surviving hospital in the country founded for the mentally ill. By 2007 the Bethel had become a residential area.

Mary Chapman is buried in the churchyard of St Andrew's church in Thorpe.

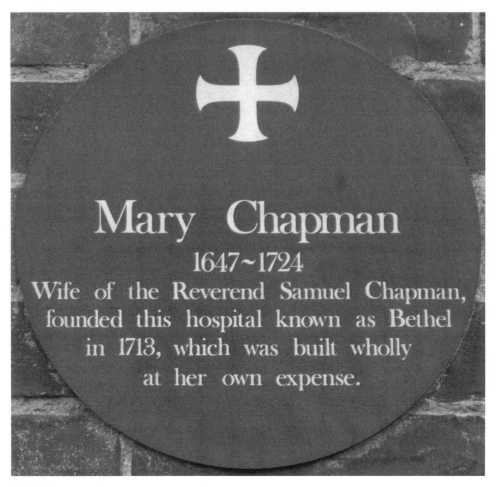

Mary Chapman plaque.

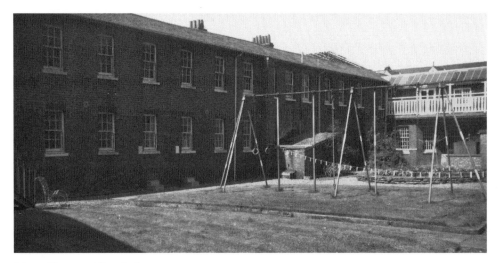

Mary Chapman Hospital.

Clarkson, Mabel (1875–1950)

Mabel was born at the priory in Calne, Wiltshire, on 1 June 1875 to solicitor Richard and his wife Elizabeth Ann. Privately educated in Reading, by the early twentieth century she was settled in Norwich.

In 1904 Mabel stood as a Liberal candidate and was elected a member of the Norwich Board of Poor-Law Guardians for Ber Street Ward, which she continued until 1925. By 1911 she looked after unemployed women through the Norwich's Distress Committee.

By 1913 Mabel was elected a Liberal councillor for Town Close Ward of Norwich Borough Council, and for some time she was the only woman in council chambers. She was appointed magistrate in 1922 when the office was first opened to women.

Mabel lost her seat in 1923, but was later re-elected in 1926 for Heigham Ward having joined the Labour Party. She later became Sheriff of Norwich in 1928, being the first woman and first member of the Labour Party to do so. In 1930 she became Lord Mayor of Norwich, was awarded a CBE in 1931 and became an Alderman in 1932.

Mabel retired from the Aldermanic Bench in 1948 due to ill health. She was a member of the Norwich District Visiting Association, the Norwich Office for the National Council of Women, the League of Nations Union and she was also in charge of the Norwich School Children's Boot Fund.

Mabel died at her home at Mount Pleasant, Norwich, on 20 March 1950. It was stated that the public life of Norwich was the poorer when Mabel Clarkson left it.

Colman, Ethel (1863–1948)

Ethel, a descendent of Mary Hardy, was the first female Lord Mayor of Norwich, and her sister, Helen Caroline, was her lady Mayoress. Ethel was the second daughter of mustard giant Jeremiah J. Colman and she was a director of a missionary society and one of the first women deacons at Princes' Street Norwich.

The *Hathor* is a Norfolk pleasure wherry, said to be one of only six of its kind remaining on the Norfolk Broads. Built by D. S. Halls of Reedham, it has been registered since 1966 on the register of National Historic Ships in the UK and is part of the National Historic Fleet.

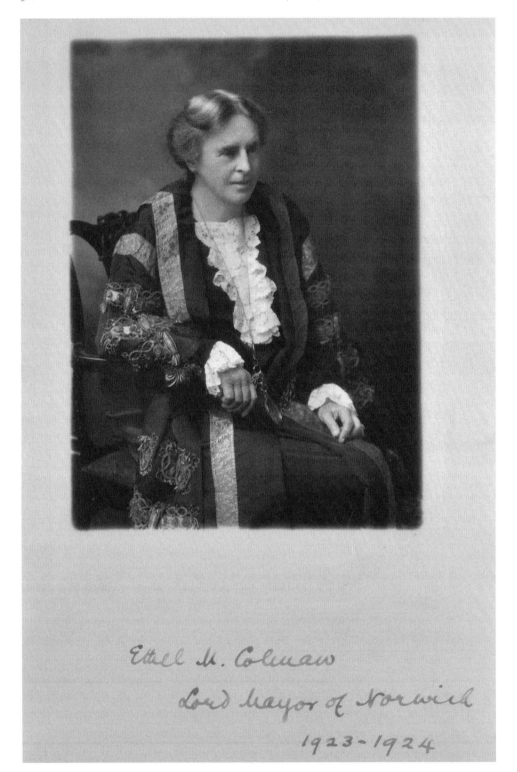

Ethel M. Colman
Lord Mayor of Norwich
1923 - 1924

Ethel Colman.

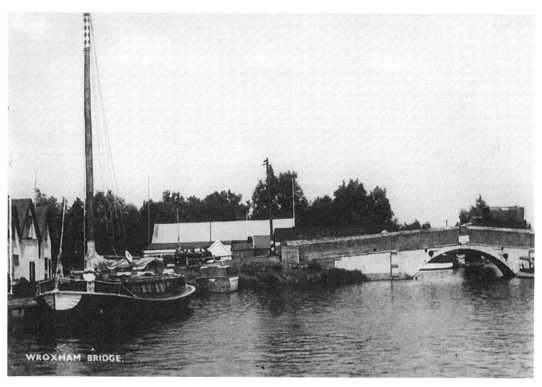

Hathor at Wroxham.

Built in 1905 for Ethel and Helen, it was named after their brother Alan who died in 1897 while on a family trip on the Nile on a boat called *Hathor*. The interior was designed by Norwich architect Edward Boardman, who was married to Florence Colman.

The Colman and Boardman family kept ownership until 1954. It was then sold to Claud Hamilton and until 1985 it was used as a house boat. The Wherry Yacht Charter Trust purchased her in an unhealthy state and undertook much-needed restoration.

In 1921 a large collection of Egyptian artefacts was donated to Norwich Castle Museum; they came with a catalogue that was commissioned by Ethel and Helen and their initials were embossed on the leather case.

Both sisters purchased Suckling House in 1923 with the view of restoring the building and opening it to the public, along with Stuart Hall. It was then given to the City of Norwich. Both sisters were involved in the welfare of the employees at the Carrow Works. Ethel also taught at the Carrow Men's First Day School and became joint-editor of the *Carrow Works Magazine*.

In 1927 Ethel became Deputy Lord Mayor to Mr Witard and was also vice-chairman of the Libraries Committee.

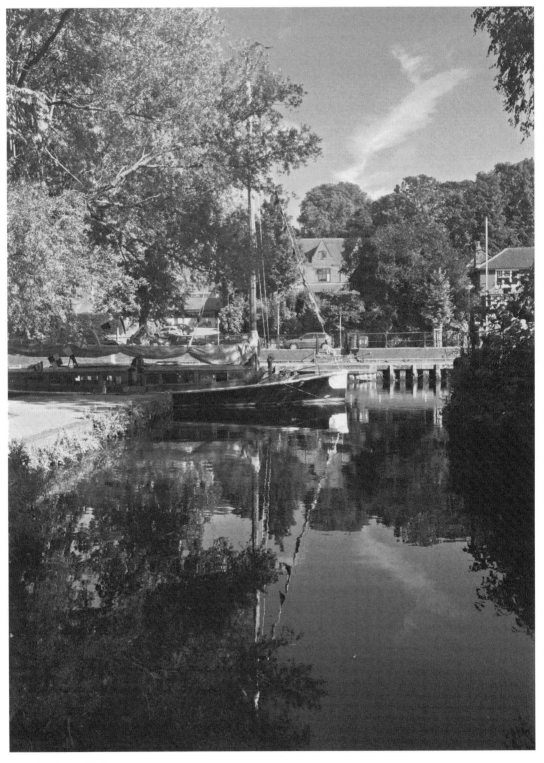

Hathor at Pulls Ferry.

Cooper, Elizabeth (burned 1557)

The Marian Persecutions were carried out against Protestant religious reformers during the reign of Mary I and they were recorded in *Foxe's Book of Martyrs*. Under Mary I the relationship between Rome and the Church of England was restored.

Lollards Pit is on Riverside Road, Norwich, and those waiting to be burnt there for their religious beliefs were held at the nearby guildhall. From there they were taken through the streets, which would normally be packed with people, but those about to be burnt at the stake were shown some form of sympathy.

At the riverbank faggots were piled high. The Church would then hand the victim over to the secular authority ready for execution.

Elizabeth Cooper, along with Simon Miller of King's Lynn, was executed for interrupting a service at St Andrews in Norwich to retract an earlier recantation of Protestantism. Just before the execution, Cecily Ormes from the parish of St Lawrence in Norwich declared her support for the two and as a result she spent a year in prison before she too was executed.

Below is the indictment (in its original format) against Elizabeth Cooper and Simon Miller:

In the Moneth of Iulye nexte ensued the Martyrdome of Simon Miller and Elizabeth Cooper. This Simon dwelling then in the Towne of Linne, a Godly and zealous man in the knowledge of the Lord and of his trueth, detesting and abhorring the contrary enforced Religiō thē set forth, came from Linne to Norwich, where he standing in the prease and hearing of the people, comming out the same time from their popish seruice ended in the Churche, began to aske them comming out of the Church The wordes of Simon Miller to the people.where he might go to haue the communiō. At which wordes diuers much maruelling to heare & see his boldnes, one that was an euill disposed Papist, hearing þe same, said: þt if he would needs go to a communion, he would go bring him thither where he should be sped of his purpose. The cause why Simon Miller was taken. Wherupō shortly after hee was brought to the Chauncellour of Norwiche (whose name was Dunning:) who after a few wordes & small talk passed with this examinate, committed him to Warde.

In the meane while as he was in examination, he had in his shoo his confession written in a certein paper, wherof a peece appearing aboue his shoo, was spyed and taken out. The Chauncellour asking if he would stand

to the cōfession of the same fayth therin conteined, he constantly affirmed
the same. Wherupō as is sayd, he was committed. Thus the sayd Simon being
in the Bishops house vnder custody of the keper there called M. Felow, how
it happened it is not certayne, whether by gentlenesse of the keper (who was
somewhat gentle that wayes) or by leaue geuē of the Bishop: or els whether he
had cōdescended of a purpose to theyr articles, Simon Miller dismissed to his
house at Linne.he was dismissed and went home to his house at Linne. Where
hee continued a certayne space, while he had disposed and set there all things
in order.

That done, he returned againe to the bishops house to his prison and keeper,
till the time at length he cōstantly abiding in his professed purpose, & defence
of Gods trueth, was by the sayd byshop and his Chauncellour cōdemned and
committed to the fire about the xiij. day of Iuly.

With this Simon Miller also was burnt one Elizabeth Coeper, Martyr.
Elizabeth Cooper (as is aforesayde) a Pewterers Wife, dwelling in Saynt
Andrewes parish in Norwich, where she had before recanted, and beyng
vnquyet for the same, and greatlye troubled inwardlye, at the last came into
the sayd Saynt Andrewes Church, the people beyng at theyr popish seruice,
and there standing in the same Elizabeth Cooper reuoketh her recantation
in the open Church.sayde she reuoked her recantation before made in that
place, and was hartely sorye that euer she did it, willing the people not to bee
deceiued, neither to take her doynges before for an example. &c. These or
suche like woordes she spake in the Church. Then cryed one Bacon. [In the
1563 edition, Foxe records that Cooper was denounced by one 'Master
Marsham' as well as Bacon. 'Marsham' was almost certainly Thomas
Marsham, a catholic alderman of Norwich. This reference to Marsham was
dropped in the 1570 edition, probably because of pressure from Marsham or
his family or friends.]

The Shrieffe agaynst his will enforced to lay handes vpon Elizabeth Cooper.
This Shiriffe (named M. Thomas Sutterton) & she had bene seruauntes
together before in one house, & for the frendship he bare vnto her, & the
more for the gospels sake he was very loth to do it, but that he was inforced
by those other persons (before specified) much against his owne cōscience,
which he now earnestly repenteth. This good woman being condemned, and
at the stake with Simon Miller to be burnt, when the fire came vnto her, she
a little shronke thereat, with a voyce crying once, ha. When the sayd Simon
Miller hearde the same, he put his hand behinde him towarde her, and willed
her to bee strong, and of good cheare: For good sister (said he) we shall haue

a ioyfull and a sweete supper. Elizabeth Cooper strengthned at the stake by Simon Miller. Whereat she beyng, as it seemed thereby strengthened, stoode as still and as quiet as one moste glad to finish that good worke whiche before most happely shee had begonne. So in fine she ended her life with her companion ioyfully, committing her soule into the handes of almighty God.

Dexter, Sarah (d. 1755)

Sarah Dexter is known for her bequest to the poor of King's Lynn:

By Indenture, bearing date of 16 September 1756, between the mayor and burgesses of King's Lynn, of the first part; John Woodcock and another, chapel-reeves of St Nichols, of the second part; and Samuel Clouds and another, executors of the Will of Sarah Dexter, of the third part; reciting, that the said Sarah Dexter, by her will, bearing the dated 30 April 1753' bequeathed to the said mayor and burgesses 150l., in trust, that the interest thereof should be distributed in the manner thereinafter mentioned, and desired that her Will should be entered in all the future parish books belonging to the chapel of St Nichols, and that the same, as well as a list of the names of the poor men and women to whom the last distribution should have been made, should be read every Easter Tuesday at the parish meeting by the chapel-reeves; the said mayor and burgesses, in consideration of the said sum of 150l., covented to pay interest for the same on the 25th September yearly to the said chapel-reeves and their successors; and the said chapel-reeves, for themselves and their successors, covented to pay to the town-clerk yearly on Easter Tuesday, in performance of the said Will, the interest of 10l., part of the said 150l., for the reading and entering the Will in the manner above mentioned, and to distribute yearly on Michaelmas-day the interest of 140l., to the poor men living in the almshouse in Broad-street (Framlingham's), and the poor women living in St James's Hospital in King's Lynn (excepting always the respective readers there) in equal shares; and should on every Easter Tuesday; at the meeting of the parishioners in the said chapel, produce and read over a list of the poor men and women of the almshouse and hospital aforesaid, to whom the last distribution should have been made.

The yearly sum of 7l 10s. is paid by the chamberlain to the chapel-wardens of St Nicholas, who pay 3l 15s. amongst the almspeople of each of the two hospitals St James's and Framlingham's.

Dhonau, Rachel (1909–1987)

Rachel (*née* Copland) was an observation diarist between 1941 and 1942. She was born in Melton Constable to Maud Helen Copland, a lady's maid, and Leonhard Piechowicz, a chauffeur from Germany who died in 1915. Mother and daughter lived in Sheringham with Maud's parents.

Rachel gained a degree from Bedford College and also from the University of London in English, and after 1931 she trained at Oxford to be a teacher. Rachel married Ernest Ben Dhonau, known as Jakob, and they settled in London with their son Timothy before moving to Paris, where Jakob was in demand as a translator.

At the start of the Second World War the family moved back to Sheringham, and in 1941 Rachel joined the mass-observation as a volunteer contributor; she also took a clerical post at the Sheringham Food Office, which looked after wartime food regulations. By 1942 Rachel was teaching in Norwich.

Drummond, Ann (1778–1819)

Ann was the first person to be buried in the first private cemetery in England, the Rosary Road Cemetery, Norwich, which was established on principles

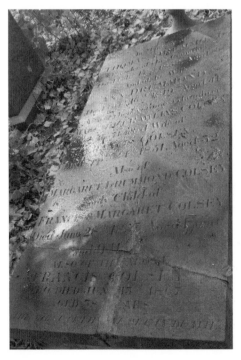

Ann Drummond's grave.

of Christian equality in 1819 by Revd Thomas Drummond, a Presbyterian minister. Ann was reinterred from the Octagon Chapel, Norwich, in 1821.

Fenn, Ida (1899–1980)

Ida Fenn wrote in the Norfolk dialect and about farming in the Eastern Counties newspapers. For twenty years Ida contributed to the *Yarmouth Mercury* with articles such as 'Tales of a Countryman' and later, 'Down on the Farm'.

Ida contributed many other articles and had two novels published that were set in Norfolk. She was born in London but was brought up in the Norfolk village of Weston Longville by her grandparents. Her first job was as a decorator, and then as an infant schoolteacher; writing was her hobby.

Ida married a farmer and they lived at Mill Farm, Winterton. In 1955 they had just purchased a farm at Hethersett when her husband passed away.

By 1973 ill health had set in, which forced Ida to stop writing the column she had written for twenty-two years. She passed away at a Lowestoft nursing home after a long illness on 1 June 1980, aged eighty-one.

Taken from Tales of a Countryman
Chapter One
US LOT

Our parish be like a lot more, there be plenty new housen gorn up ivv'ry deer, but ours, they're like they wore when Faar wooz faast marrit an can't' live there. That wooz thowt on, well, lastways thaas what he tells me.

We be tree houses in a row, all jined t'woon anourther-like. In woon and there be owld Kenyon. He be a pensioner, an he live alone. Than there be Faar an me. Faar, he teerk the pension tew, an he an Kenyon, they roam about tergather. When thaas hot, they set outside our geert on old owld tree what we cut down dicka's years ago. They like t'set there in the sun an mardle.

But at tuther and there be Besser. She be niece tew owld Kenyon, but she went an marrit Nailer, an now they're got tew little booys. Nailer, he be our willidge onder-teerker. He're got a shud down the bottom o' our gardens. Thaas where he knock up his boxes.

Besser, she's a rare good mauther. She gave us a clean up Faar an me, and she beerk us a short keerk an thart. She clean up owld Kenyon an-all. Though she dornt reckon a lot o' the jourb. She reckon thart ind smell sort o' perkewloier. Thowld cottages a stood there a lot o' years an Kenyon's ind be agin the deek, haps thaas why, else haps thaas thowld beer he drink. Thart beunt the little housen cause they're set right a-top o' the garden, all in a row like our cottages, w' tree doors all in a row. Besser seer she's glad hars be at tuther ind away from owld Kenyon's cause he dew growl an talk so when he go there, an thowld walls beunt werra thick.

Howsumarver, yow can't hev ut all ways, Woon thing we're got push-button lights, an Besser she're got a push-button oven. They did talk o'putting us a pull-cheern up our little houses, but nayther Faar n' yit Kenyon wunt sign fott. They said they wore afraid they'd be washed away woon deer when there wornt nobrer about. My gal Lucer, she seer they be a couple o' owld fules, an thart is sitch as tham what meerk ut bad fer ourthers. Lucer an me, we're bin in a cortin arver since we went t' scule, well arver since I kin remember. Folks keep a arstin when we're gorn t git marrit. Thart dew worry them so, especially owld Jesser Jones wat keep the Pust Orfuss. She's a mucka owld woman, allust a wantin t' know ourther folks bizness. She dornt git a sight out o'me, thaas why she meerk a germ o' me affront o' folks when I go in arter Faar's barker. If I wooz t' be like some and tell har all the gossip, she'd hully meerk a fuss o' me. Like my meert Queena hew I wark wuth, his owld gal go an dew a bit o' scrubbing, an she teerk owld Jesser all the news, an bring away anourther fresh lot. Pore owld Queena, he hev a life ont w' owld Ranner. Thaas what I seer, they tork about Lucer an me gitten marrit, how'd I know but what she mightn't go an tarn out t' be anourther Ranner an start a orderin me about. As I seer, we're good frens apart an though we're had our neerms down fer a rare wild, I beunt in no hurrer t' teerk on a wife an thaas a fack. Faar, he seer he oont hev us live along w'him, cause he like his house t' his saalf, an Lucer's owld gal seer the seerm. She reckon thart wunt be long afore the house'd be alive w' kids a creerzin the life out on'er. So like thart, ye see, though folks here an there about the parush git ideas ivvery so orfen. Lucer and me still be like we wore years ago.

Look a thart there mauther Jiffler, she're bin gorn t' git marrit hunnets o' times. Har sister, she narver blew ut about, she up an slipped off t' Yaarm'th a Jiffer, an cam' back a Shucka with a riddy-meered fambly – well not far ouf ennerway, an she're bin in a muddle arver since Queena Seer, "Jess yow wait, partner. There be plenty time fer yow yit." But Lucer keep on about anourther year gone ivvery time Christmas come round, and how much longer be us messing about. No doubt woon deer suffen'll happen, an there nobrer ont

want t' wonder any longer. As thing are, when Lucer git har rile up. I kin up
and go back t' Faar.

Flowerday, Philippa (c. 1872)

In 1872 mustard company J. & J. Colman employed thirty-two-year-old
Philippa Flowerday as the first-ever industrial nurse in Britain when wages
were 26s a week. Having trained at the Norfolk and Norwich Hospital,
her duties at J. & J. Colman were to assist the doctor every morning and to
take supplies from the works kitchen to the sick at home, which led to up to

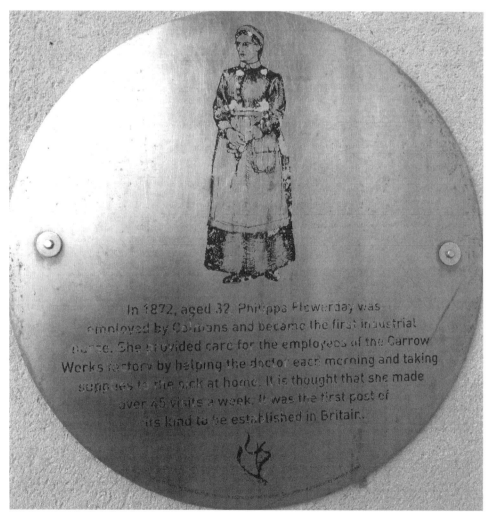

Philippa Flowerday plaque.

forty-five visits per week. Philippa helped to set up the Colman's Sick Society and a clothing club. In 1888 Philippa married Colman's head gardener and her duties were continued by Nurse Quarry.

Fountaine, Margaret (1862–1940)

Born in Norwich on 16 May 1862, Margaret was a Victorian lepidopterist and diarist. She was the eldest of seven children born to Revd John Fountaine and Mary Isabella Lee. She had a great knowledge of butterflies and she travelled through Europe, South Africa, India, Tibet, America, Australia and the West Indies. Her specimens, which numbered over 22,000 and are housed as the Fountaine-Neimy Collection at the Norwich Collection Museum, were mostly bred from eggs or caterpillars.

Margaret was a well-travelled woman, collecting in sixty different countries in fifty years and becoming an expert in tropical butterfly life-cycles. By 1978 there were twelve large volumes of her works with over 3,203 pages. Her four sketchbooks of butterfly life cycles are held at the Natural History Museum in London. Margaret died in Trinidad.

Aged twenty-seven, Margaret and her sisters became financially independent and she became infatuated with Septimus Hewson, an Irish chorister at Norwich Cathedral. He was later dismissed through drinking and it was soon clear that no marriage would take place. She felt that she had been ill used.

In 1895 she met botanist and entomologist Henry John Elwes, and this led to a visit to Sicily where she started her own collection.

During 1901 she visited Damascus and met with Khalil Neimy, who became her guide and translator. He went on to become her companion even though he had a wife. Their affair lasted for twenty-seven years and ended only with his death from fever on 7 July 1928. In that time they travelled to Algeria, Spain, the Caribbean, Central America, Near East, Far East, Turkey, India, USA, Fiji, New Zealand, West Africa and Queensland in Australia to search for butterflies.

The British Vice-Consul at Broussa threatened Margaret with a breach of promise suit after she broke the engagement she had agreed to in 1905. She returned to England in 1925 and she put together a large studio at Fellowes Road, Hampstead; she then travelled intensely and buried herself in her work.

Margaret died in 1940 aged seventy-eight, suffering a heart attack on the slopes of Mount St Benedict in Trinidad. She is buried in an unmarked grave at Woodbroke Cemetery, Port of Spain, Trinidad.

A note left in her diary regarding Septimus Hewson 1889 reads:

Before presenting this – the Story of my Life – to those whoever they may be one hundred years from the date on which it was first commenced to be written, i.e. April 15: 1878, I fill it incumbent upon me to offer some sort of apology for much that is recorded therin, especially during the first few years, when (I was barely 16 at the time it was began) I naturally passed through a rather profitless and foolish period of life, such as was and no doubt is still, prevalent amongst very young girls, though perhaps more so then – a hundred years ago when the education of women was so shamelessly neglected, leaving the uninitiated female to commence life with all the yearnings of nature quite unexplained to her, and the follies and foibles of youth only too ready to enter the hitherto unoccupied and possibly imaginative brain.

Some writer has said (I think it is Bulmer Lytton) that 'a woman's whole life is a history of the affections – the heart is her world'. And indeed, there is alas! Much that is only too true in this statement, for are not these loves, so fondly cherished and so dearly clung to, often merely as it were so many gates leading on, through paths of sorrow, to ultimate disaster and final loss?

The greatest passion, and perhaps the most noble love of my life was no doubt for Septimus Hewson, and the blow I received from his heartless conduct left a scar upon my heart, which no length of time ever quite effaced,

For Charles Neimy, whose love and friendship for me endured for a period of no less than 27 years, ending only with his death, I felt a deep devotion and true affection; and certainly the most interesting part of my life was spent with him. The dear companion – the constant and untiring friend and assistant in our Entomological work, travelling as we did together over all the loveliest, the wildest and often the loneliest places of this most beautiful Earth, while the roving spirit and love of the wilderness drew us closely together in a bond of union in spite of our widely different spheres of life, race and individuality in a way that was often quite inexplicable to most of those who knew us.

To the Reader – maybe yet unborn – leave this record of the wild and fearless life of one of the 'South Acre Children', who never 'grew up' & who enjoyed greatly and suffered much.

M. E. Fountaine

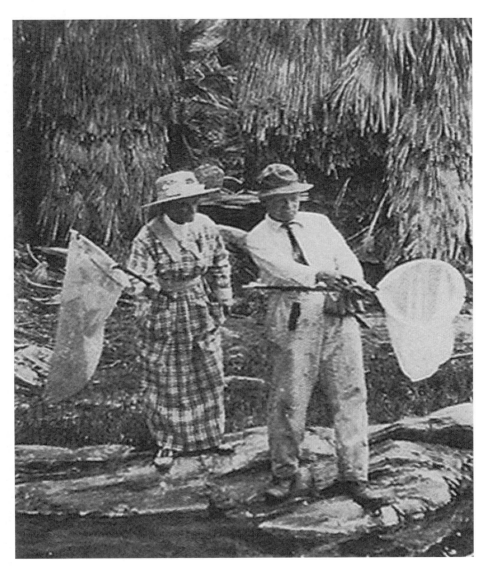

Margaret Fountaine.

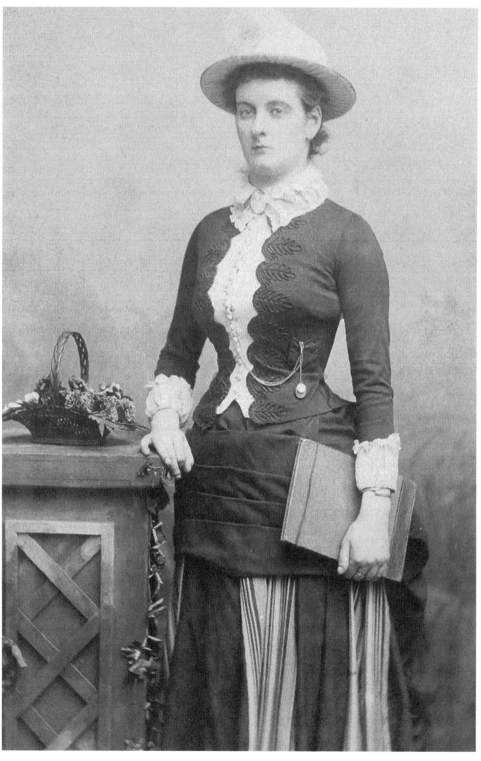

Margaret Fountaine.

Fry, Elizabeth (1780–1845)

Elizabeth Betsy Fry (*née* Gurney) was a Quaker, Christian philanthropist, social reformer and prison reformer who was often referred to as the 'angel of prisons'. She was born 21 May 1780 at Gurney Court, which is off Magdalen

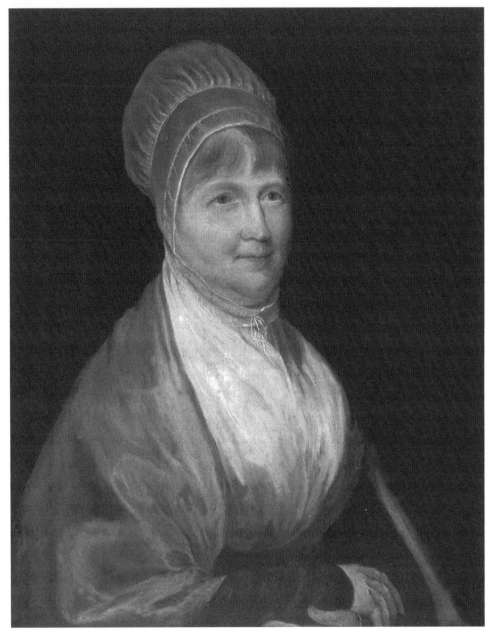

Elizabeth Fry.

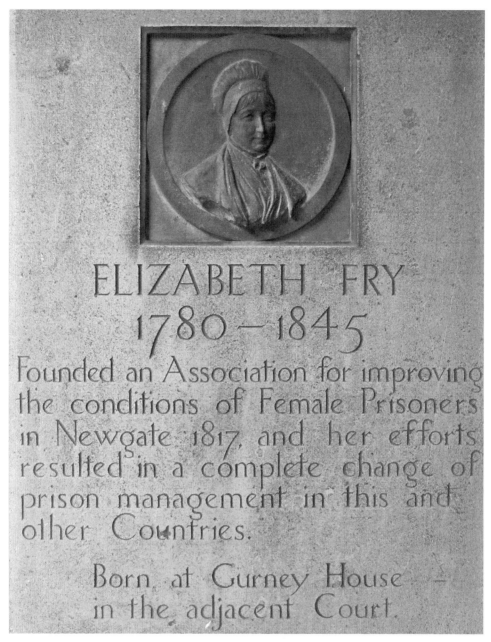

Elizabeth Fry plaque.

Street, Norwich, and her childhood home was Earlham Hall, which is now part of the University of East Anglia.

Her father John was a partner in Gurney's Bank and her mother Catherine was a member of the Barclay Family, founders of Barclays Bank. As her mother died relatively young, Elizabeth took up the role of bringing up her siblings.

At an early age Elizabeth took to reading the preachings of American Quaker William Savery, and it was because of Savery's words that Elizabeth took an interest in prisoners, along with the ill and poor. She also set up a Sunday school during the summer months to help children learn to read and write.

At the age of twenty Elizabeth met the Quaker and banker Joseph Fry and they were married on 19 August 1800 at the Friends Meeting House, situated at Goat Lane, Norwich. They then moved to St Mildred's Court in the City of London. From the years 1809 to 1829 the couple lived in Upton Lane, Forest Gate, East London. They had five sons and six daughters.

When Elizabeth visited Newgate Prison, which was situated near the Old Bailey, she was completely shocked by what she saw, especially with how the women and children were being housed. She started to visit constantly, bringing food and clothes for some of the prisoners. By 1816, Elizabeth founded a prison school for children who were imprisoned with their mothers. By 1817 she went on to co-found the Association for the Reformation of the Female Prisoners in Newgate, which went on to create the British Ladies' Society for Promoting the Reformation of Female Prisoners – the first nationwide women's organisation in Britain.

Elizabeth and some invited nobility stayed in some of the prisons to see what conditions were like, which helped with her writing. Elizabeth's brother-in-law Thomas Foxwell Buxton became MP for Weymouth and he started to promote her works. Elizabeth became the first woman to give evidence to a House of Commons committee on British prison conditions.

The reforms advocated by Elizabeth had three core ingredients:

1. Male and female prisoners had to be accommodated separately and guards had to be of the same gender as the prisoners. This has since become standard international practice.
2. Arrangements for regular visits to female prisons were established and, in addition, the volunteers had to take care of education, paid work and support after their clients left prison.
3. Prisoners were to have opportunities for education and paid work.

Elizabeth went on to establish a night shelter in London, and in 1824 in Brighton she set up the Brighton District Visiting Society and visited, along with volunteers, the poor to offer help. This was soon duplicated all over Britain.

By the year 1840 Elizabeth set up a training school for nurses, which inspired Florence Nightingale, who went on to take a team of nurses to the wounded in the Crimean War.

In 1842 Frederick William IV of Prussia was so taken by the work that Elizabeth had done in prisons that he met her in Newgate Prison.

Elizabeth died after suffering a stroke while in Ramsgate on 12 October 1845 and is buried at the Friends' burial ground at Barking, Essex. Although normally only reserved for the death of a ruling monarch, the seamen of the Ramsgate Coast Guard flew their flag at half-mast.

Following her death, a property was purchased at No. 195 Mare Street in Hackney, London, and opened as a refuge in 1849. By 1924 the refuge joined the Manor House Refuge for the Destitute in Dalston, Hackney, becoming a hostel for young girls on probation. In 1958 it moved to Reading.

Hidden treasures of Elizabeth's were found in an attic chest at Northrepps Hall in Cromer. The items included a fragile red notebook with handwritten notes about prison conditions, which was placed on display at the English House Gallery at Norwich Castle Museum during the first half of 2009.

Many prisons have a memorial to Elizabeth, and since 2001 her face has been shown on the back of the five pound notes issued by the Bank of England, although by 2016 it will have been replaced by Winston Churchill.

Frye, Kate (1878–1959)

From 1911 to 1914 Kate Frye spent more than twenty weeks working with the New Constitutional Society for Women Suffrage's campaign based in East Dereham, which took place at a house in Commercial Road, East Dereham. The house was owned by a widow called Mrs Alice West, whose youngest daughter Hilda also lived there. Mrs West decided to let out two rooms. Kate took one of the rooms, but when it was not possible to stay there Kate resided nearby at Norwich Street with widow Mrs Martha Cox.

At the Dereham branch of the London and Provisional Bank, Kate met with bank manager Charles Corey and on 9 May 1912 Kate set up a society, the Coreys' daughter Violet being made honorary secretary.

It was a year previous in Dereham that Kate arranged her first public 'Votes for Women' at the eighteenth-century Assembly Rooms. An entry in her diary of 22 March 1911 reads,

> I was over at the hall at 7. We opened the doors at 7.20 and in very little time the place was full. I had to stand at the door and kept the youths and maidens out till the police officer arrived and then went up to sell the literature.

Kate sharply arranged another public meeting on Wednesday 12 June 1911. Her diary states, 'Miss Corey sold tickets downstairs and I was the door keeper and spoke to everyone coming in.'

The main speaker was the Revd Hugh Chapman, who was joined by the Revd Harold Davidson, rector of Stiffkey, who would later go on to be known all over England.

Gabley, Mother (d. 1583)

Mother Gabley was arrested for witchcraft, having caused the deaths of Robert Archer, Oliver Cobb, William Barret, Richard Dye, Henry Gouldsmith and others who were coming to England from Spain (they drowned west of the harbour). The parish register, based at Wells-next-the-Sea, shows the recording of the verdict of a jury relating to the death of thirteen individuals who had been drowned:

> Misled uppo' ye Weste coaste coming from Spain; whose deaths were brought to pass by the detestable working of an execrable witch of King's Lynn; whose name was Mother Gabley; by the boiling, or rather labouring of certain eggs in a pailful of cold water:- afterwards proved sufficiently at the arraignment of the said witch.

Mother Gabley is the earliest reference of a witch being condemned in Norfolk under the 1563 Act.

Glover, Sarah (1786–1867)

In 1841 Revd John Curwen was tasked by the conference of teachers at the Sunday School Union with finding a suitable way to teach music in Sunday schools. A friend showed him the work of Sarah Glover, that being the *Scheme to Render Psalmody Congregational*. Revd Curwen derived the works that became known as the Tonic Sol-fa System of notation.

Sarah Glover was born in Norwich in 1786. Her father was the rector of St Lawrence church. She was given music lessons, starting on her sixth birthday, and she became an accomplished pianist. By the time Sarah was in her twenties she was in charge of music at her father's church. Other churches

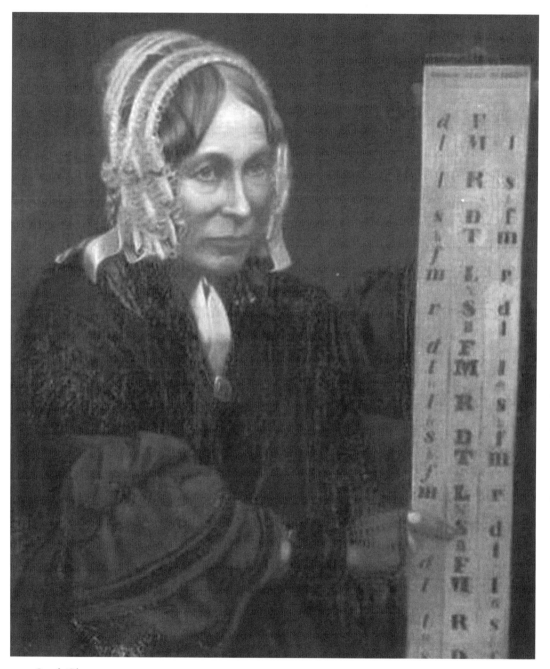

Sarah Glover.

in the area were sending their children to Sarah with the view of being given singing lessons.

Sarah first attempted to teach music when she saw her sister Christina attempting to drum a tune into the head of the Sunday schoolteacher on the piano. She set about placing labels on the keys of the piano, leaving the teacher pick out the notes of the song for himself along with the help of an alphabetical notation.

Soon Sarah set out the sol-fa-syllables (D, R, M, F, S, L, T) and this gave her the idea to work on the traditional notation. The four alternative notations were as follows:

1st   The inadequate representation of the scale of the staff, no difference being made between the whole and the half notes.

2nd   The encumbrance of non-accidental sharps and flats which embarrass the practice and perplex the theory of music, rendering some keys much more abstruse than others, though the construction of all of them in equally simple.

3rd   The confusion arising from the contrivance of clefs, by which device characters varying in appearance are used to express identical names and sound.

4th   The needless variety (in some instance) complexity of characters employed to represent notes, differing in nothing except the octave where they occur. For example, observe the entire absence of analogy in the representation of five out of the six C's on the piano-forte.

Sarah soon started to train several children using these methods, which soon became known as the Norwich Sol-fa Ladder.

Sarah later felt the need to invent an instrument that could provide harmonic support when a piano was not available. The instrument invented was a dulcimer, made of glass resonators and equipped with a movable chart of the sol-far initials, called a glass harmonica. The scales were as follows:

Doh ra me fah sol lah te	= diatonic
Lah ted oh ra me fah soh	= minor
Lah ted oh ra me ba ne	= melodic minor
Doy roy moy foy soy loy toy	= chromatic sharps
Doy row mow fow sow low tow	= chromatic flats

The rhythmic notation started with a capital letter followed by a lowercase letter to indicate the duration with every additional letter, and by 1839 the notation was changed for the use of hyphens.

The History of the Norwich Solfa System was published anonymously in 1844 and there is only one copy in existence – housed at the Tonic Sol-fa College of Music in England as the property of the estate of John Curwen.

What caused a problem with Sarah's system was the use of her unique notation. One of the pupils stated, 'I believe, that the old and new notations were totally at variance.' Although the Tonic Sol-far System was created by Sarah, it is John Curwen who over the years has been credited as being its originator. After looking into the way Sarah set it up, Curwen understood why his attempts as a child to read music had failed. He started to teach Sarah's methods to a young child and found that within two weeks Curwen was able to read a psalm-tune written in the solfa notation.

The following is the first letter that Curwen sent to Sarah:

Stowmarket
Oct. 4, 1841

Dear Madam,

For it is to a Lady, I think, that I address myself; I hope you will excuse the liberty I take in writing to you, though unknown, concerning the Solfa System of Musical Notation.

Early in the Spring of this year Mrs Reed visited several of the schools in Norwich. She was particularly interested to perceive the facility with which children taught on your method, learnt to read music. She kindly lent me your books, 'The Scheme for Rendering Psalmody Congregational 'and 'The Solfa Tune Book,' and informed me of the surprising effects which they had produced. I studied them with deep interest, for during the time which I spent at Basingstoke I had taken great pains for a long time in teaching children to sing. We used Mr Hickson's 'Singing Master' and had two hundred children in the Singing meetings twice a week. But there are so many puzzling preliminary things to be taught, according to the old notation before we reach Interval, and that is so uncertain a thing (unless a child can carry the signature along the staff) – never decided by half a tone, that we were unable to make any real progress.

I am persuaded that your method is not only practically efficient, but that a child taught by it will possess a more thorough knowledge of the Theory of music than half the country choristers in the Kingdom.

Lately journeying in the north I have had opportunities of recommending the Solfa system very strongly. But I recommended it with some alterations in regard to the mode of presenting it to the eye. These I think important; and it is due to you that I should mention them.

1st., I would use only the small letters, and indicate the octaves above and below by figures thus; d d^1 d^2. Transition (Modulation) into a key a fifth from the Tonic should be marked by Italic letters which point to the right. Transition into a key fourth from the Tonic by letters leaning backwards, pointing to the left.

It is difficult for the eye to alter its focus suddenly and frequently as in the change from Capital to small letters.

Secondly: although the analogy you mention of the arrangement of the prismatic colours – with the divisions of a monochord – is very interesting, yet, as we do practically treat Do as the Tonic – the first note of the scale, both in the Table of Tune and in your exercises on the common chord – I cannot yield up its right to Lah. Making Lah the first note in the diatonic scale when we practically treat Do as such only puzzles the beginner.

Thirdly: As it is not probable that the point notation [staff notation] will be superseded for instrumental music, and as the common instruments will generally be used for pitching (or giving the keynote) – would it not be better to indicate the pitch notes by the letters of the common notation?

Fourthly: Merely for the sake of more distinct marketing and convenience of printing I would express the aliquot parts of a Measure thus ! : ; and would cause the same space on the paper to be given to each aliquot or Beat.

Fifthly: For dividing a beat I think you would find the following signs useful. –

To signify that the note preceding fills half a beat

To signify that the note preceding fills a quarter of a beat

To signify that the note preceding fills three quarters of a beat.

I feel the more anxious to inform you of these things, because, before I felt so strongly convinced as now I am of the importance of these improvements, - I had advertised to print a little Tune Book for children in the Solfa notation, and now I feel whether you will permit me to call it by that name when it has undergone so many changes, But I have only altered its outward form. The principle and the whole idea of the thing remains the same.

I have been engaged to write articles on Sabbath School Education for a periodical which will be published next year. I should like to be able to print music in it; thus to introduce solfa notation to a wide circle of those who must require it.

I should be anxious till I hear from you on this subject; if indeed I may presume to ask such a favour from one to whom I am unknown.

The notation as thus altered with specimens of tunes will accompany this.

Believe me, dear Madam, Yours with sincere respect,

John Curwen

Sarah was very much opposed to any changes and many letters were written between Curwen and Sarah, and the following is a letter to the press from someone who was at one stage employed by Sarah Glover:

Letter to the editor of the Norwich Mercury
April 26, 1879
Miss Glover's Sol-Far Notation
To the Editor

Sir,

In your issue of Wednesday, the 23rd inst., there is a letter signed 'Tonic SolFa' in which the writer says Miss Glover was a consenting Party to the change made in her system by Mr Curwen. This I can most confidently deny. Her consent was never asked at all. I was at the time employed by Miss G to teach her system in the Norwich Schools, and was in consequence very frequently at her house in Chapel Field Grove. I remember Mr Curwen coming from London and getting an introduction to Miss G., and how she made him welcome to her house, and took him to the school in the Black Boys Yard, St George's and taught him her system, under a promise from him and Colonial Schools, with which he was, or pretended, to be connected. I remembered after his return to London she waited several weary weeks before she heard from him. But one evening I called on business, and before I left she said, 'Oh! I have heard from Mr Curwen at last.' I was pleased to hear it, and said: 'May I ask what account he gives of his progress in introducing it in London?' For an answer she put into my hands a large envelope, which contained a musical ladder, a fac-simile of Miss Glover's with this difference, where she had capital letters he had Roman small; where she had Roman small, he had italics; and where she had italics, he had Old English. There was also a little book of school songs in the letter notation with the same alterations. When I looked at the contents of the envelope I was thunderstruck, and sat staring at them Miss Christiana, who was more impulsive than her sister, suggested, and using an ephithet, that he ought to be prosecuted. 'Richly, richly!' I exclaimed. When Miss Glover said,'Oh sister, sister; hold your tongue, and remember we should forgive our enemies, and pray for those who despitefully use us'. Turning to me she said, 'I must say I am greatly pained at this breach of confidence, but with God's help I will get over the pain'.

I have a letter from Miss Glover, dated December 13th, 1858, in which she says, in reference to some business matters, 'I advise you not to communicate it to others, for sly opposition seems to me to be so prevalent in these days, that one need beware how one publishes an idea that may suggest an opportunity for counteracting a prosperous plan'.

Miss Glover's musical ladder consisted of three columns, the middle column always represented the tonic or key of the tune being practised, the right hand column the dominant, and the left hand column the sub-dominant; thus if C was the tonic, G was the dominant and F the sub-dominant – s D f.

Mr Curwen's first ladder marked thus – s d f.

Miss Glover never intended her system to supersede the common notation, but as an introduction to it, for in her book called a 'Scheme to Render Psalmody Congregational,' published by Jarrold and Son, Norwich, you will find the set of diagrams, which on a large scale were the table of time, the table of degrees and the table to which the pupils were regularly drilled till they could sing from the common notes as easily as they could from the sol-fa, and visitors to the school frequently brought tunes and wrote them on the black board to test their proficiency. The diagrams were the table of the time, the table of degrees and the table of tune. The Government Inspectors' reports were very favourable to the plan of teaching laid down by Miss Glover. In hopes you will find room for this,

I am Sir, respectfully yours

J. B.

Curwen continued to write to Sarah for over twenty years in the hope of gaining her endorsement of his modifications, and just before her death in 1867 in Great Malvern from a stroke it seems that there was some mutual respect between the two.

The system is today most famous as a song from the film *The Sound of Music*.

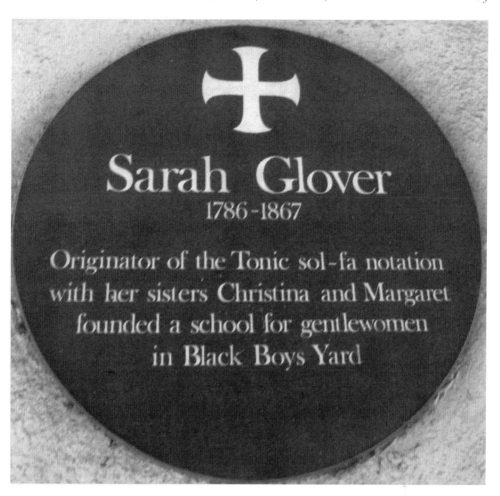

Above: Sarah Glover school plaque.

Right: Sarah Glover home plaque.

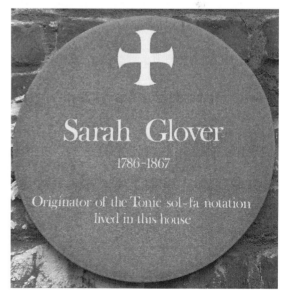

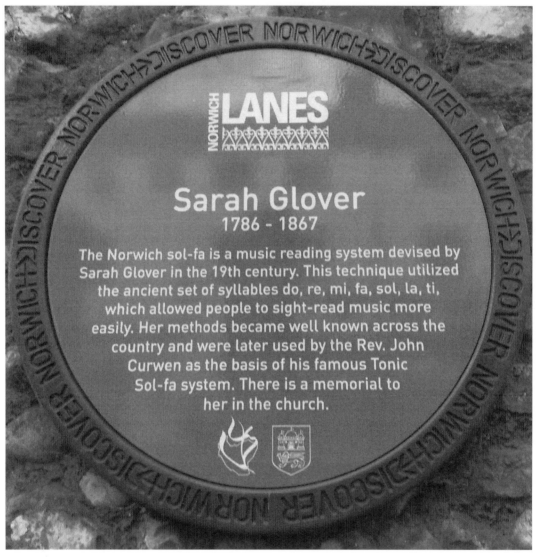

Sarah Glover church plaque.

Gunhilde (d. 1002)

Gunhilde, whose name could also be spelt Gunhild, is alleged to have been the sister of Sweyn Forkbeard, who was the King of Denmark. The reason for this is because in the entry for Sweyn in the *Oxford Dictionary of National Biography* there is no mention of Gunhilde, although she is given a mention in the *Chronicle of John of Wallingford*. She was the daughter of Harald Bluetooth and was married to Pallig the Dane, who as ealdorman of Devonshire served under Æthelred the Unready, King of England.

History states, but does not confirm, that Gunhilde was taken hostage in England and then murdered in the St Brice's Day massacre that was ordered by Æthelred. Her husband Pallig is also said to have been murdered there for deserting the service of the King. If the case is true it would answer the question as to why Sweyn invaded England in 1003, with the eventual conquest being led by his son Cnut.

Gurney, Anna (1795–1857)

Anna, a British scholar, was a member of the old, established Gurney family. She was the youngest child of Richard Gurney and his second wife Rachel of Keswick Hall, Norwich. Aged only ten months, Anna was struck down with a paralytic affliction. She spent the rest of her life an active person who was not able to stand or to move without mechanical aid.

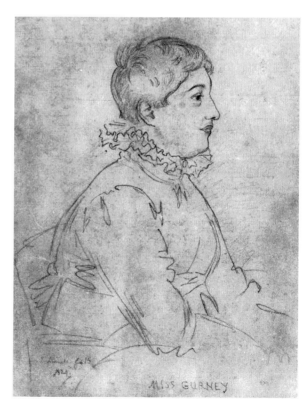

Anna Gurney pencil portrait.

Anna learnt many languages, including Latin, Greek, Hebrew and Anglo-Saxon, and in 1819 she brought out anonymously for private use a book called *A Literal Translation of the Saxon Chronicle, by a Lady in the Country*.

After her mother died, Anna went to live with Miss Sarah Buxton at Northrepps Cottage near Cromer, which is now Northrepps Cottage Country Hotel. Miss Buxton died in 1839 and Anna continued to live there.

At her own cost she purchased a Manby's apparatus for saving lives of seamen in difficulty on dangerous coasts. She was escorted to the beach in times of urgency to direct all operations from her chair.

Anna kept an active life and worked with the author Amelia Opie. The two of them created an anti-slavery society in Norwich. After visiting Rome, Athens and Argos in 1845, Anna became the first lady to join the British Archaeology Association.

Still having an unquenchable thirst for knowledge, Anna went on to read Danish, Swedish and Russian literature. Anna died at the home of her brother

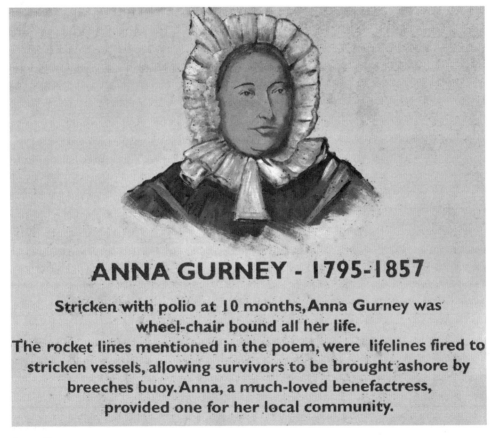

ANNA GURNEY - 1795-1857

**Stricken with polio at 10 months, Anna Gurney was wheel-chair bound all her life.
The rocket lines mentioned in the poem, were lifelines fired to stricken vessels, allowing survivors to be brought ashore by breeches buoy. Anna, a much-loved benefactress, provided one for her local community.**

Anna Gurney grave stone.

Hudson at Keswick on 6 June 1857 after a short illness and was buried in Overstrand church.

Gurney-Hoare, Louisa (1784–1836)

Louisa was born on 25 September 1784, the seventh child of John Gurney of Earlham Hall and Catherine Bell. Her father owned Gurney's bank in Norwich and one of her sisters was Elizabeth Fry. All the children were educated at home, and although brought up as Quakers, they did mix with and have friends with Unitarian and Roman Catholic beliefs.

All of the Gurney children were encouraged to keep journals. Louisa documented an incident that induced great disgust, which was that of her twelve-year-old-cousin kissing her. However, she did go on to marry said cousin, Samuel Hoare, on 24 December 1806 at Tasborough Meeting House. In 1812 husband and wife were baptised into the Church of England and they moved into a house in Hampstead, London, purchased by Samuel's father.

Louisa went on to join the anti-slavery campaign led by her brother-in-law Sir Thomas Foxwell Buxton and also the prison reform movement that was led by her sister Elizabeth Fry and her husband. In 1825 she founded the 'Ladies Society for Promoting Education in the West Indies', which had the support of the Gurney, Hoare, Buxton and Ricardo families.

Although Louisa was heavily supportive of the society, her main focus of campaign was education, and her book *Hints for the Improvement of Early Education and Nursery Discipline* was written in 1819 for the nursemaid of her six children. The book sold for over eighty years. Louisa's second book, *Friendly Advice on the Management and Education of Children, Addressed to Parents of the Middle and Labouring Classes of Society*, was written in 1824 and was produced mainly for schools with the statement 'preserve children from evil, not from childishness'. The final book, called *Letters from a Work-House Boy*, 1826, was reprinted many times by the Religious Tract Society.

Louisa died in Hampstead on 6 September 1836.

Hall, Catherine Edith (c. 1895–1900)

Catherine was a diarist during the late nineteenth and early twentieth centuries who lived in Southery, 11 miles north of Ely. She started her diary in 1895 and concluded it in 1900. The contents covered settling into the parish, renovations, parish work, social visits, and shopping.

Hannent, Antoinette (1905–1976)

Antoinette (Antonetto Carrara), better known as 'Black Anna', was born in Ber Street, Norwich, and was of Italian heritage. Her mother Lizabetta came

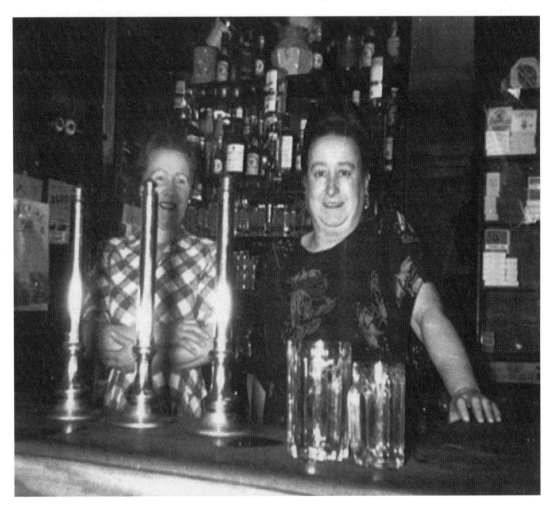

Antoinette Hannent.

to Norwich in the 1880s and was known as 'lovely Liz'. She married Kenneth Jack Hannent, who became landlord of the Jolly Butchers in September 1935. Kenneth died in April 1947 and Anna ran the pub until she died in May 1976.

Anna was very considerate to her gay clients, especially in a period when homosexuality was against the law. She also ran the last Common Lodging House in Norwich, otherwise known as 'doss-house' – the local police used the services of this building when the cells were full.

Anna was an amazing singer of jazz and became more interested in jazz and blues when, during the Second World War, American soldiers were billeted to the pub. She went on to be known as 'the English Sophie Tucker', and

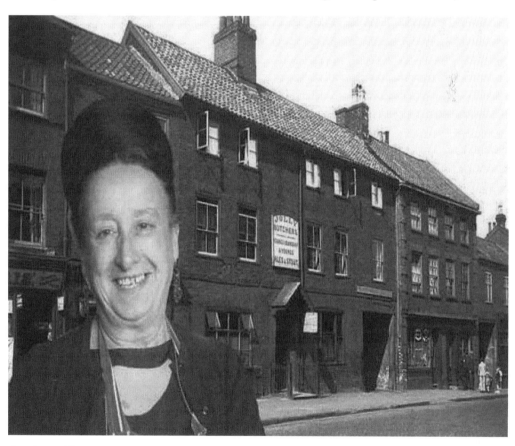

Antoinette Hannent.

she played a foot-pumped harmonium. She hated electronic music and never had a microphone in the pub – everything was acoustic.

Anna sang with Acker Bilk, Chris Barber and Tony Lighthouse, and when Danny la Rue was filming in Norfolk he gave a party for Anna.

A hard but fair lady; if anyone stepped out of line she would use her copper laundry stick to shepherd them out of the pub.

Anna's reputation was such that she could no longer sing in the pub as sometimes there would be over eighty people present – too many to cram into the place. Anna did however play the big Earlham Park jazz festivals. Along with

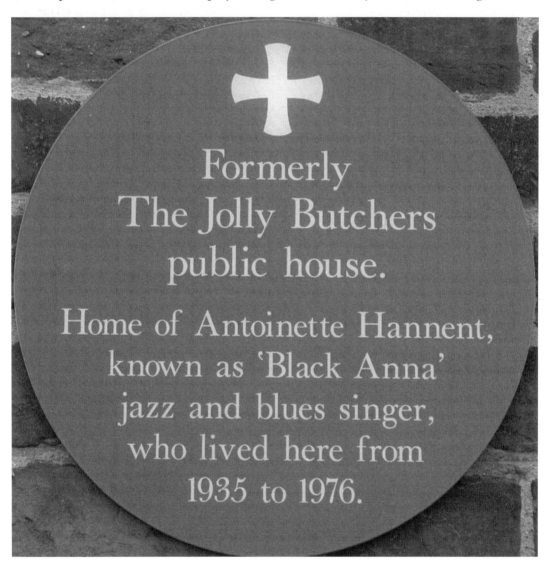

The Jolly Butchers plaque.

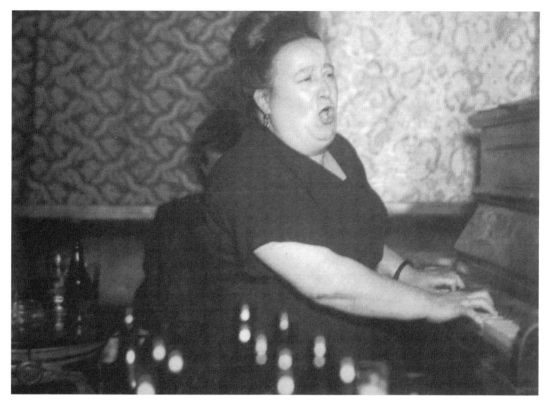

Antoinette Hannent in action.

Albert Cooper she formed the Jolly Butchers Skiffle Group, which went on to become the Albert Cooper Folk Group by 1960/61.

In February 1976 Anna fell over on snow and died three months later.

The Jolly Butchers would continue into the 1980s as an underground reggae club and soul club, before closing in 1989 to become offices.

Hardy, Mary (1733–1809)

Mary spent her whole life living in Norfolk where she wrote her daily diary, first at Coltishall, Norwich, from 1773 to 1781 and then at Letheringsett, near Cley, from 1781 until her death in 1809.

Mary's diary chronicled the activities of her family and those that worked on the family's farm, maltings and brewery. The writings, if not known, could have been styled by her husband William Hardy; in fact the opening entry states a reference to Mary's recovery after the birth of daughter Mary Anne when aged forty. It also reads, 'Went to Church after Lying in 3 Weeks & 4 days.'

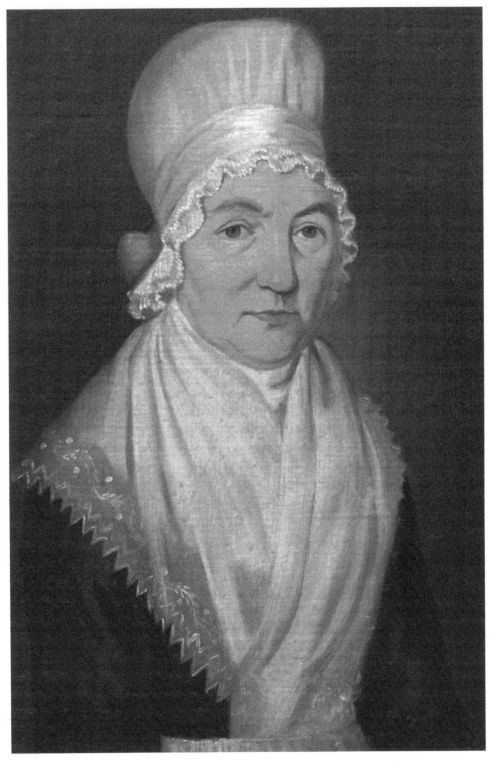

Mary Hardy.

Her husband William possessed the vote and exercised it in favour of Foxite Whigs candidates in many elections. Both Mary and William were literate and numerate, and they had great influence in the commercial world. They travelled, visiting Lincoln, Hull, York, Lancashire and London.

By 1774 the entries have more of a human tone, talking about the children, friends and people from work. Mary also took an interest further afield, choosing subjects such as taxes, politicians, bankruptcy and war, both on sea and land.

Back at work, Mary continues to write about ploughing, sowing, malting, orders and payments.

In the thirty-six years of her diary, Mary went from being an Anglican to being both Anglican and Nonconformist to being exclusively a Nonconformist. She even stopped doing what she once enjoyed – dancing, theatre and cards. In 1798 she became a member of the Wesleyan Methodist in Cley, which she attended with her son-in-law Jeremiah Cozens, a Calvinistic Baptist.

Mary's diaries were contained in five ledger books. The early entries were written by William with Mary dictating. Over a period of thirty-six years the ledger books contained some 570,000 words.

Hare, Sarah (d. 1744)

It was said that Sarah Hare's death in 1744 was punishment for sewing on a Sunday; she pricked her finger, with the probably consequence being blood poisoning.

What is amazing about Sarah is her lifelike wax effigy, which is the only statue of its kind in England outside of Westminster Abbey.

Sarah was the daughter of Sir Thomas Hare of Stow Hall in Stow Bardolph, in which the Hare family had lived since 1589. Sarah's will dated August 1743 states the following:

> I desire six of the poor men in the parish of Stow or Wimbotsham may put me in to the ground they having five shillings a piece for the same. I desire all the poor in the Alms Row may have two shillings and sixpence each at the Grave before I am put in. This I hope my Executor will see firstly performed before Sunset … I desire to have my face and hands made in wax with a piece of crimson satin thrown like a garment in a picture hair upon my head and put in a case of Mahogany with a glass before and fix'd up so near the place were

my corps lyes as it can be with my name and time of Death put upon the case in any manner most desirable if I do not execute this in my life I desire it may be done after my Death.

During the year the will was made, Sarah had moulded impressions made of her face and hands. She was buried in the Hare mausoleum in Holy Trinity Church. A cabinet housing her life-size effigy states the words 'Here lyeth the body of Sarah Hare.'

On having seen this life-size effigy, it is a bit of a shock to the system. Only visible are the torso – dressed in one of Sarah's gowns – head and hands, and a dark curly wig. The face clearly shows painted skin blemishes and warts.

In 1987 Sarah's effigy was restored by Judith Dore and Monica Dance, and they described the following during their restoration:

> The wax surface was cleaned with a mild soap to remove dirt; cracking was stopped by lining of the head with an open weave material dipped in molten wax. A thin layer of water colour was then applied to give a more life-like appearance. For the costume, a highly skilled conservationist was required as it was in such bad condition. The cabinet housing the effigy was damaged and rodents had gained access and eaten part of the costume. The cabinet was also repaired.

Harrod, Wilhelmine (1911–2005)

Wilhelmine Margaret Eve Harrod (*née* Cresswell) (Lady Harrod) (Billa), an architectural conservationist, was born on 1 December 1911 at New Hunstanton, Snettisham. Her father was Lieutenant Francis Joseph Creswell of the Norfolk Regiment, killed in action at Mons and Billa's mother Barbara remarried to General Sir (Edward) Peter Strickland.

Because the family moved around a lot, her stepfather's postings being peripatetic, Billa was privately educated, which included time spent at the Sorbonne in Paris.

Billa later became a wardrobe mistress working for many London film studios. By the 1930s she became engaged to the poet John Betjeman. Although they did not marry, they did remain lifelong friends.

She later met Roy Harrod (later Sir Henry Roy Forbes) and they were married on 8 January 1938 at St Mary's church, Snettisham. They then went to live in Oxford where Billa would entertain clients of her husband along with friends – it was stated that Nancy Mitford based the character of Fanny in *Love in a Cold Climate* on her.

In later years Billa took a keen interest in the conservation movement, and along with Charles Linnell she wrote *The Shell Guide to Norfolk* in 1957.

When her husband retired they moved back to Norfolk, settling in Holt where they purchased the Rectory. By 1970, thirty-two medieval churches faced demolition, and Billa, who was a devout Anglican, gained the support of lifelong friend Sir John Betjeman. She founded the Friends of Norwich Churches and in 1976 she became the founding chairman of the Norfolk Churches Trust. In 1972 she wrote *Norfolk County Churches and the Future* with illustrations by Osbert Lancaster and John Piper and the introduction was by Sir John Betjeman.

Billa took Prince Charles on what she declared a 'church crawl' and he became patron of the trust in 1989.

Billa was appointed the OBE in 1992 and she died on 9 May 2005 at the family home at Holt.

Higdon, Kitty (Annie Catherine) (1864–1946)

Kitty (*née* Schollick) was born on 30 December 1864 in Cheshire. She was the daughter of a foreman shipwright called Samuel and his wife Jane. Kitty trained to be a teacher, taking posts in Somerset and London. She went on to marry fellow teacher Thomas George Higdon on 11 July 1896.

The couple first lived and worked in London before they took up joint posts on 14 April 1902 at Wood Dalling Council School. Kitty was employed as the head teacher and Thomas as an assistant. Both were Christian socialists and they strived to improve the conditions at the school, being most concerned about the way the children were being employed illegally by local farmers.

The main problem the couple came up against was that the majority of the farmers were also school managers and they did not like the idea that the Higdons were encouraging the farmworkers to join trade unions. This caused so much tension that the Norfolk Education Committee gave the Higdons the choice of dismissal or to work at another school.

Not wanting to be dismissed, the couple took up positions at the Burston and Shimpling Council School on 1 February 1911.

Revd Charles Tucker Eland became chairman of the School Managing Body and his main aim was to recover all the powers that the Church had lost to the parish councils.

It was not long after the Higdons arrived that their concerns led to arguments with the school managers. Thomas had worked with local farmers to help remove sitting members at the parish council elections, with himself being head of the poll, and in 1913 Norfolk Education Committee were requested by the school managers to remove Kitty from the position she held on disciplinary grounds. Kitty refused and as a result she and her husband were dismissed on 31 March 1914, even though the school inspectors made it very clear that Kitty was a most excellent teacher. But just before this, Tom stood for election to the parish council and topped the poll, beating Eland, who came bottom.

On the 1 April 1914, school pupil Violet Potter led sixty-seven out of seventy-two pupils on strike to show their support and loyalty to the Higdons. Most of the parents refused to send their children back to the official Council

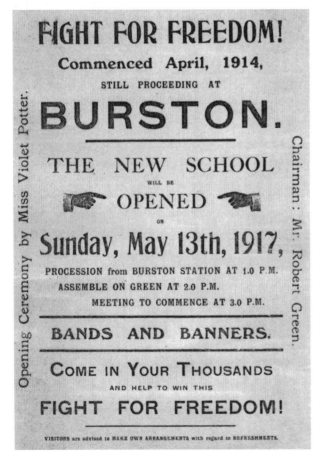

Strike poster.

School and instead set up the Burston Strike School, which at first was held outside on the village green until a room was given above the carpenter's shop in Burston.

As weeks went by the strike drew the attention from trade unions and labour organisations. Meetings were held on Burston Green, with speeches being given by leading political figures. A national campaign took place to build a property to use as a school, and it opened on 13 May 1917 with Sylvia Pankhurst attending.

The School Management Committee staged a plan of attack and eighteen parents were summoned to court for refusing to send their children to school. The fines were paid from a collection made outside the courts. By the first year of the strike the Labour Party raised over £1,250.

During the 1920s and 1930s the school not only took in local children, but children far and wide, including the children of members of the Russian Trade Delegation who were in London. The building was later described by the Higdons as the 'centre of a new living movement of educational and social activity'.

Thomas died in August 1939 and the last eleven pupils were relocated to Burston Council School. Kitty took to retirement at a home at Swainsthorpe, where she died on 24 April 1946. Both are buried in Burston Churchyard.

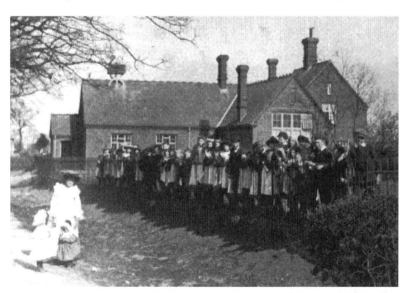

Strike!

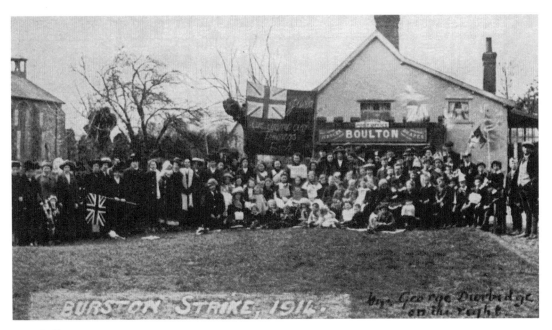

Strike!

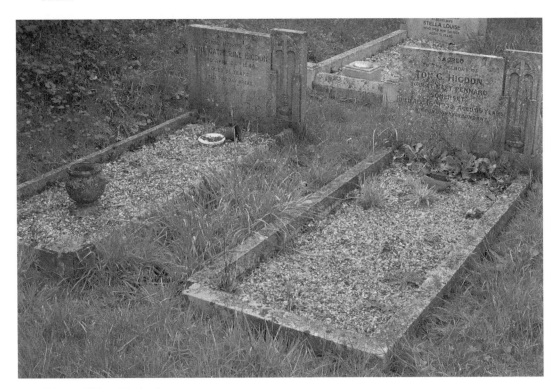

Kitty and Tom Higdon's graves.

Today the school is a museum, and on 1 September every year since 1984 the Transport and General Workers' Union and others commemorate the school and the strike as being the longest strike in the UK.

In 1985 the story was dramatised by the BBC, called *The Burston Rebellion*, which starred Eileen Atkins as Kitty, Bernard Hill as Tom, John Shrapnel as the Revd Eland and Nicola Cowper as Violet Potter.

The boycott earned its place in history as the longest-lasting strike ever.

Howes, Ena (b. 1919)

Ena Howes (*née* Mallett) was born in 1919 and raised in Kessingland. She studied at Lowestoft Secondary School and at sixteen became a post office counter clerk and telephonist at Methwold, which is where she met her future husband Frank (married September 1940).

At the start of the Second World War, Ena joined the Wrens and after one year working as a clerical officer on HMS *Granges*, she was given the post as a telephonist. Soon promoted to Leading Wren, she was moved to HMS *Beaver* in Grimsby, by 1943 to HMS *Raven* at Eastleigh, Hants, and then promoted to Wren Petty Officer.

Ena soon moved to Fort Southwick, Portsmouth, where her position was one of overall charge of the telephone exchange at the D-Day headquarters.

The 4 August 1944 saw Ena become one of the first six Wrens to go to France as Admiral Ramsay's telephonist until he passed away in January 1945. Ena also served in Germany until demobbed in December 1945, also having been awarded the British Empire Medal in June that year.

In the 1990s, Roy Larking recorded an interview with Ena:

I left the Lowestoft Secondary School at the end of the Christmas Term in 1935, when I was sixteen. I had to stay on for one term of the new school year because my birthday was in August and the rule then, was that you could only leave that school at the end of the term following the sixteenth birthday. Had I been at any other school in Lowestoft or Kessingland I could have left when I was fourteen. I had decided while still at school, that I would try to include travel in my job specification so I wrote to the Cunard Line, to find out what jobs were available on a liner and how would you train to

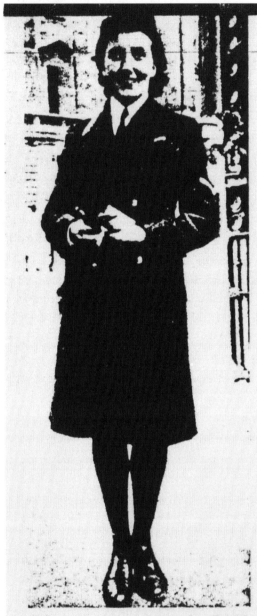

Bobby Howes receiving the British Empire Medal from King George VI.

Ena Howes receiving the British Empire Medal.

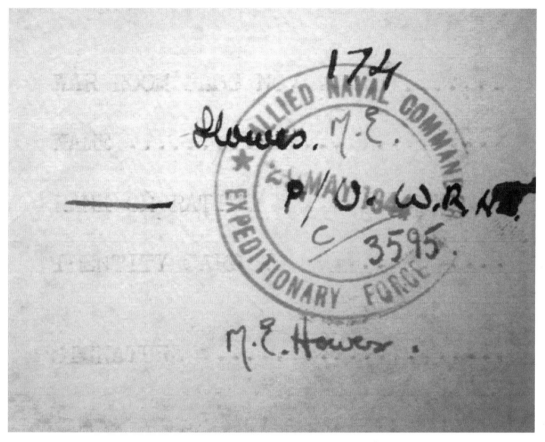

Ena Howes badge.

qualify for such a job, little knowing, that if I got the position. I would have been sea-sick most of the time!! The reply stated that a woman had to be a minimum of twenty-five years old, to be accepted as a crew and that the main vacancies were as stewardesses. I did not fancy that because I imagined the passengers being sick a lot of the time and I did not relish the thought of clearing up after them.

Hairdressing was on offer, but that was a non-starter also. However, when I saw 'telephonist', I knew that my job skills must include, and so straight away, my application for consideration for an apprentice telephonist, was on its way to the telephone exchange in Lowestoft.

Unfortunately, the manager at the exchange, Mr Glasscock, treated my application, less favourably than I had hopped. The job needed a high degree of concentration, and so the operators, worked four-hour shifts: four on, four off. One day a girl worked from eight until noon, and again from four until eight in the evening. On the next day, she worked from noon until four.

Mr Glasscock considered the rest period between noon and four, and decided that I would not be able to cycle to Kessingland and back (in all weathers), between the two shifts and so, did not offer me the job.

During my 'interview' time at the Telephone Exchange, I learned that they often recruited people in the telephone Exchange from Sub-Post Offices and so my second application for an apprenticeship, was to Kensington Road Post Office, Pakefield, and this was successful.

I was taught Post Office counter work by Phyllis Spurgeon, the Postmaster's daughter. My apprenticeship there, was for one year, and at the end of that time, (as so often happened in the thirties), I was out of a job, because a Postmaster could not afford to pay a qualified counter clerk.

My next 'foray' was a course of shorthand and typing at Madame Benson's in the High Street in Lowestoft but I soon decided that that was not for me and so got a job at Eastern Coachworks at Lowestoft. The work entailed, entering by hand on to sheets of paper, all the stores as they were drawn by the workmen and the work was so boring, that I knew that I couldn't stay their either.

At that time, there were no really good jobs available, unless you stayed on at School. And it was by very good luck that the Rector of Kessingland, the Reverend Emms, heard possibly through a Church Magazine, that there was a vacancy for a Post Office Counter Clerk-cum-telephonist at Methwold Post Office, north-west of Brandon in Norfolk. The fact that the Post Office there, had a telephone exchange, appealed to me and so I applied and was accepted.

At that time, my longest excursion from Lowestoft, was a day trip to Norwich and so it would be quiet an adventure, to go to Methwold, especially on my own but my burning desire to train as a telephonist, gave me the necessary impetus.

From Ena Howes, in her own words:

Whilst on leave from my post as a Wren telephonist on 23 March 1944, I received a telegram instructing me to go to Fort Southwick, Portsmouth for an interview for a mystery job. Although I was successful and was given the job, I still had no idea what position was to be filled.

On 1 April 1944, I duly reported to Southwick House in the small village of Southwick in Hampshire. The house was at the end of a long drive and on arrival I was directed to the cellar where a large telephone exchange was being constructed by two GPO engineers.

I was soon to find out how important this place was when I started constructing a telephone directory. I found that General Eisenhower, General Bradley, General Montgomery, Admiral Ramsay, Rear Admiral Creasy and Air Chief Marshal Tedder all had telephones on the exchange.

To keep the telephone exchange secret we answered calls using the code word 'SK'. Our postal address was Naval Party 1645 c/o BFMO Reading and no postage was required for mail but 'On Active Service' was written on the envelopes and all letters were censored. We were also allowed out in a 10 mile area of Southwick House.

When the Wren telephonists arrived we all did two weeks' training at Fort Southwick, a Combined Ops Exchange, and 150 steps underground in a series of tunnels. We had to practise using a VHF telephone that had one-way transmissions. This came in useful when Winston Churchill visited the troops in France after D-Day and made a call to King George VI from this telephone on the beach. Then I had the task of explaining to the King's secretary that he had to say 'over to you' before the other person could speak.

As the Royal Navy is the senior service I was put in charge although the exchange was manned by an equal number of Wrens and Royal Corps of Signals men of 21st Army Group. I wrote out the Duty Roster and kept them in order. Telephonists were not allowed to take cups of tea on to the switchboard and there was no smoking permitted but they were allowed short breaks in an adjoining room.

I had a desk at the back of the Exchange and had to make Visual Index Files for each of the 16 positions on the exchange.

The telephonists worked 24 hours, 7 days a week and were divided into three watches to cover the day and night duties. I only worked days but Army corporals were in charge when I went off duty.

There was a small 10 + 50 telephone exchange in the War room so I had a War Room pass to visit and supervise my Wren manning this exchange. A Royal Marine with a rifle was on duty at the door to see that nobody else was allowed in except the top brass and the Wren plotters. In the War Room, as well as a wall map which had been made from Chad Valley, the jigsaw makers, there was a map of the coasts of Britain and France on a table where the plotters worked moving models of ships and aircraft and men as instructions came through their headphones.

Unwittingly, the arrival of the naval officers caused me a headache when some of them didn't like the rooms they were allocated and changed with other officers. This made my directories useless and I was allocated Sgt

Lever from the Royal Corps of Signals to help sort it out. He went to the various rooms and rang me to say who was on each extension. So an accurate directory could finally be made and visual index files for each operator brought up to date.

We were always busy answering calls with no time to chat. The switchboard was a mass of small lights that glowed individually when a call came in. The most important people had blue lights when they made a call and the second in importance had red lights while the majority had white lights. The officers with blue lights also clear the line facilities which meant we could interrupt a call if it was engaged when they needed it. They also had scramblers and when asking a call they would ask 'can you scramble'. This meant that the words they were saying were inintelligible without a scrambler device at one end and sounded like Donald Duck so were very secret. As D-Day approached one Wren was heard to say 'the exchange was lit up like Blackpool illuminations'.

We had been called to a meeting the day before D-Day when the weather was too bad to sail and Admiral Ramsay arranged a cricket match between the officers and Wrens. When one Wren had difficulty batting, he changed from bowling over-arm to underarm to give her more chance of hitting the ball. It reminded Admiral Creasy of the Armada before which Drake played bowls on Plymouth Hoe.

The weather was not ideal on 4/5 June 1944 but at the meeting in the War Room on the eve of D-Day, the Met officers advised that it would be two more weeks if the invasion was cancelled before the tides and moon were right for the landing. So General Dwight Eisenhower famously said 'let's go' and the invasion of France was on.

I stayed on duty all night on the 5/6 June 1944. General Omar Bradley was the first to call to say that they had a foothold on OMAHA beach. Unfortunately, as later became clear, this part of the coast was heavily defended and the Americans suffered heavy losses.

When I went to breakfast in the Nissen hut, which was our mess in the morning we waited for the BBC 9am news to make an announcement of the landings and a big cheer went up when the nation heard that we had a foothold in France. We had been part of it!

The Royal Corps of signals man telephonists all departed to France and life became much quieter until the middle of August when the first Wrens left for France. I was in the advance party of three to leave, to set up communications.

The photograph accompanying memories was in the Evening News at Portsmouth, which said 'The first Wrens leave for France.'

We went across to Arromanches in a destroyer, then in a 15cwt open backed truck across Normandy to Granville. We couldn't sail down the west coast of Normandy as the Germans were still in the Channel Islands a few miles away. As the roads had been bombed by the Allies we arrived in a very dusty state and couldn't wait to get washed. Until the main party arrived we lived in a French guesthouse and had meals with the American GIs in the casino which was great as their food was good.

When we were told the main party would be arriving we had to move into an empty medieval village called Hauteville, which the Germans had vacated after D-Day. Unfortunately the main party didn't arrive as there were U-boats in the English Channel and they were not allowed to sail. So we chose a three story house in the village and barricaded ourselves in a top bedroom by placing our large kitbags against the door. We slept on the floor, fully dressed, with our gas masks for pillows and our duffle coats for blankets, and were very happy to see the main party arrive next day.

We stayed in Granville until 12 September when we moved to La Celle St Cloud, just outside Paris, where we were billeted in two long wooden huts in the grounds of the Chateau. They were divided into cabins, a few individuals and others holding five bunks. There was an ablution room at one end with a row of toilets and a row of washbasins with only cold water taps. Fortunately our Quarters PO, Wren Dorothy Harvey, was able to obtain a field kitchen copper, which we could fill with cold water and heat by lighting a fire underneath. There was plenty of wood in the grounds of the Chateau. We had a canvas bath fitted into a wooden frame and this we set up on the floor. It was very draughty with Wrens coming to wash or visit the toilets and no privacy so we didn't bathe very often.

When the weather worsened and winter set in, we were snowbound and the journey by truck from La Celle St Cloud to the Chateau d' Hennement where we worked in offices became hazardous. On Christmas Day 1944 we made a fire in the mess in a wrought iron stove and broke up a chair to get it started, as the wood in the grounds was so wet. That was the worst Christmas I've ever had. On 1 January 1945 I was asked to report to Admiral Ramsey's office where he informed me that my name was in the New Year's Honours list. I had been awarded the British Empire Medal, Military Division, for zeal and wholehearted devotion to duty.

Unfortunately, the next day, 2 January 1945, Admiral Ramsey was killed in an air crash. His plane crashed on take-off as he was leaving with his staff officer (Operations) for a staff meeting in Brussels. Whether it skidded in the snow or the weight of the snow on the wings caused the crash was never divulged but we were all desperately sorry to lose such a popular admiral. We attended his funeral in the new cemetery at St Germaine en Laye and were allowed to wear Wellington boots with our bell bottom trousers tucked in because of the snow. As the cemetery is opposite Chateau d' Hennement where we worked, we walked there behind the main party. General Eisenhower came in his jeep with his outriders on motor cycles wearing white helmets, white gauntlets and white gaiters. We called them the snowdrops. All the top people from the Army, Navy and RAF attended.

By February the snow was so deep and the roads so frosty, the truck we were in almost skidded of the hill at Bougival into the river below. And we were eventually moved into a house in St Germaine en Laye, where I shared a room with PO Dorothy Harvey, our Quarters Petty Officer, and we actually had a washbasin with hot and cold water on tap, such luxury.

On 8 May 1945 when VE Day was announced, we went into Paris to celebrate with the French people who crowded down the Champs Elysees. The excitement was immense.

In June the advance party moved to Minden in Germany. We were supposed to fly, but when we arrived at Le Bourget airport the planes couldn't take off because of fog. As our kit had already left by Royal Marine Lorries, we had to return to base and share with the main party. It was either a canvas bed or a mattress on the floor. We left the next day by single decker bus driven by Royal Marines and were given 24 hour survival packs. Tea was in a cube with milk and sugar, just pour hot water on it. We had little methylated spirit stoves to heat the water by the side of the road when we stopped for a comfort break. Wrens went over the hedge one side of the road and Royal Marine drivers the opposite side. We stayed in a hotel in Brussels overnight then continued our journey to Minden the next day.

We arrived in time for our evening meal which was spam, peas and potatoes, followed by tinned peaches. We were in the American zone which meant most of the food was in tins. However, our irons (knife, fork and spoon) were in our kitbags which hadn't arrived so we had to eat peas and peaches with our fingers – very slippery. We were billeted in houses which were in an area commandeered by the army and surrounded by rolls of barbed wire, with a Royal Marine sentry on duty at the road entrance. We worked in a factory in the area which was taken over and were fortunate enough to have an open air swimming pool in the grounds. We were not issued with German money as we were not allowed to go out in the town so didn't need it, whereas in France we were paid in francs to spend in Paris.

The only time we went to Minden was after VJ-Day when we had a service of thanksgiving for victory in the local church.

I flew home to attend an investiture at Buckingham Palace on 26 June 1945 in a Dakota aircraft from a tiny airfield called Buckeberg and was given a week's leave. King George VI asked me how long I had been in France then pinned the medal on my Wren's jacket and then I was free to continue my week's leave.

On VJ-Day the navy ordered 'splice the main brace' and we were all given a tot of rum in our enamel mugs, with disastrous effects on some of the Wrens.

I was given my discharge in December 1945 and went home by train and boat, a long miserable journey, to be at home for Christmas 1945, but because I was owed so much leave, I wasn't actually discharged until February 1946.

Jewson, Dorothy (1884–1964)

Dorothy was the daughter of Alderman George Jewson, a coal merchant, and his wife Mary Jane Jarrold, born on 17 August 1884. The family were from 'Braema' on Thorpe Road, Norwich. Dorothy's father was in charge of the family-run business and during her teens the family moved to the grander Tower House in Bracondale. She was christened Dorothea but never used the name, and was educated at Norwich High School for Girls, which was housed in the Assembly House. In 1903 Dorothy went to Cheltenham Ladies' College and then Girton College, Cambridge. She then went on to become a teacher, firstly with the girls' boarding school, West Heath School, Ham Common, Kingston in Surrey. Dorothy stayed there until 1911 where she joined a former board school in Norwich. It was at this stage that she joined the WSPU, the militant suffragette group led by the Pankhursts.

Dorothy's name can be found on many reports of activities in Norwich for support of women's suffrage. A meeting took place in Norwich Market Place on Sunday 28 July that Dorothy had helped to organise; her brother Harry presided on a few of the platforms.

One of the helpers was Miriam Pratt who was a Norwich schoolteacher. Miriam set fire to two empty buildings in Cambridge and the Jewsons came to look after her. Harry put up the bail and Dorothy the defence fund.

With her brother Harry she looked into poverty in Norwich and published *The Destitute of Norwich and how they live: a Report into the Administration of our Relief* (1912). She was a member of the Fabian Society, which she found did not suit her, and she joined the Independent Labour Party. Harry was killed at Gazza on the 19 April 1917 and Dorothy was left with Pankhursts, who were pro-war.

During the First World War Dorothy helped to run training centres for unemployed girls under the age of seventeen and she was soon put in touch with trade union leader Mary Macarthur to become an organiser for the National Federation of Woman Workers in London (NFWW). When this merged with the National Union of General and Municipal Workers in 1921, Dorothy became employed by the women's section. As a pacifist she was against Britain's involvement the First World War.

Dorothy was elected Labour MP for Norwich during the 1923 General Election, one of three women to be elected – the others were Margaret Bondfield and Susan Lawrence. Dorothy was a very active MP, speaking out on female and family issues. Her maiden speech was about extending voting rights to young women and she gained more influence for Labour women within their own party's structure. The seat was lost one year later and Dorothy never returned to Parliament. Both Margaret and Susan also lost their seats, but did return; in fact, Margaret Bondfield went on to become Britain's first female cabinet minister in 1929.

Dorothy was a member of Norwich City Council from 1927 to 1936. Married to Richard Tanner Smith, they went to live in Goodmayes, Essex. Richard passed away in 1939, and Dorothy went on to marry Campbell Steven in 1945, an MP for Glasgow Camlachie who passed away in 1947. For a long period of time Dorothy lived at Orpington in Kent.

In the 1920s she joined and was an active member of the No More War Committee. Her pacifism drew her to the Society of Friends and she was admitted as a member of the Croydon and Southwark meeting in 1958. The following is taken from the manifesto of 1924:

Parliamentary Election 1924

Polling Day, Wednesday Oct 29th

Labour will continue to fight for the uplifting of the people.

To the Electors

Fellow Citizens,

The defeat of the Labour Government by the combined vote of the liberals and conservatives in the House of Commons left the Labour Party no option but to appeal to the country.

The Norwich Labour Party has again honoured us by an invitation to be their candidates and it is with even greater confidence than before that we appeal for your support.

The record of the Labour Government during its brief term of office is one that must command the confidence of all who wish to see social well-being at home, and peace and goodwill among the Nations ahead

[The manifesto then goes on to talk about Armaments, Russian Treaty, Unemployment, Old Age Pension, Ex-Service Men, Education, Housing and Health and Finance and Taxation before continuing:]

The wider views and accomplishments of the Government on these and many other questions such as Mothers' Pensions, Hours of Labour, Workmen's Compensation, Franchise, Agriculture, Social and Industrial Reconstruction are stated in the Manifesto issued by the Labour Party, which we hope to place in the hands of every Elector.

As citizens of Norwich Having close contact with, and knowledge of all local aspects of these great questions, and because of the proved fitness of Labour to hold office, we ask for a renewal of the confidence given to us in December last.

Yours faithfully,

DOROTHY JEWSON

WALTER R SMITH

Guildhall Corner Chambers

Norwich

The last months of her life were spent in a cottage in her brother Christopher's grounds in Lower Hellesdon, and it was here that she passed away on 29 February 1964, aged seventy-nine. Her funeral service was held at the Friend's Meeting House, Norwich, and she went on to be cremated at St Faith's Crematorium.

Julian (c. 1342–1416)

Julian of Norwich was an anchoress and was also known to be a Christian mystic. Her book *Revelations of Divine Love*, which was written around 1395, is the first book in English to have been written by a woman.

At the age of thirty, Julian became very ill, and while on her deathbed she believed she saw a vision of Jesus Christ which only ended when she fully recovered from her illness on 13 May 1373. Although it took some years to complete the text, each vision was written about after they had taken place, and a part of the book known as *The Short Text* has a narrative of twenty-five chapters.

Up to thirty years later Julian started to write a theological text of the book known as *The Long Text*, which had eighty-six chapters. It was stated that Julian was visited around 1414 by the mystic Margery Kempe.

The Short Text was not edited until 1911 and *The Long Text* is still the better-known part. The one surviving manuscript is the late fifteenth-century Westminster Manuscript which contains part of *The Long Text* and which told the world that Julian was its author. The first printed version was edited by Serenus Cressy, a Benedictine monk in 1670, and it later had reprints in 1843, 1864 and 1902. In 1877 a modern version of *The Long Text* was published by Henry Collins, and in the 1901 publication by Grace Warrack introduced early twentieth-century readers to the works of Julian. The book was translated into numerous languages.

The legacy of Julian continues to live on with Julian's feast day in the Roman Catholic tradition falling on 13 May; it also falls on 13 May in the Anglican and Lutheran traditions. The song 'Julian of Norwich' ('The Bells of Norwich') based on the words of Julian was written by Sydney Carter in 1981. The Julian Study Centre was set up at the University of East Anglia in 2013. From the same year there have been week-long celebrations in Norwich to help to show the significance of Julian, and there is also a stained-glass window of Julian with a cat in Norwich Cathedral.

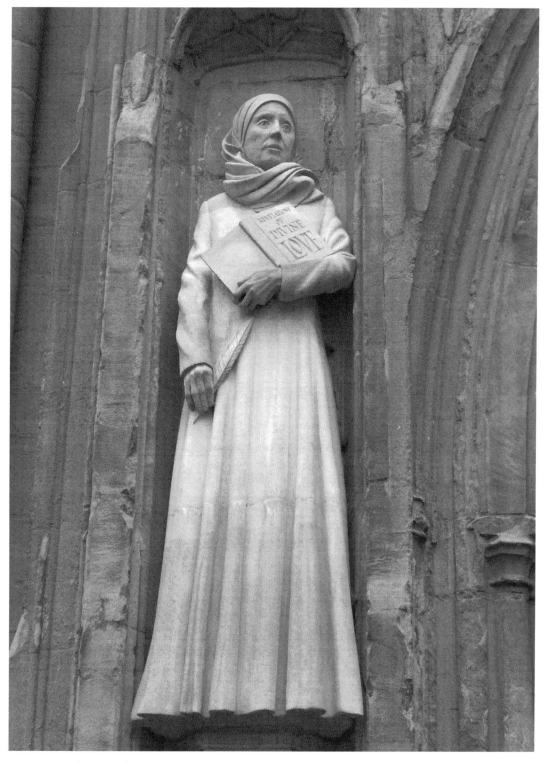

Statue of Dame Julian.

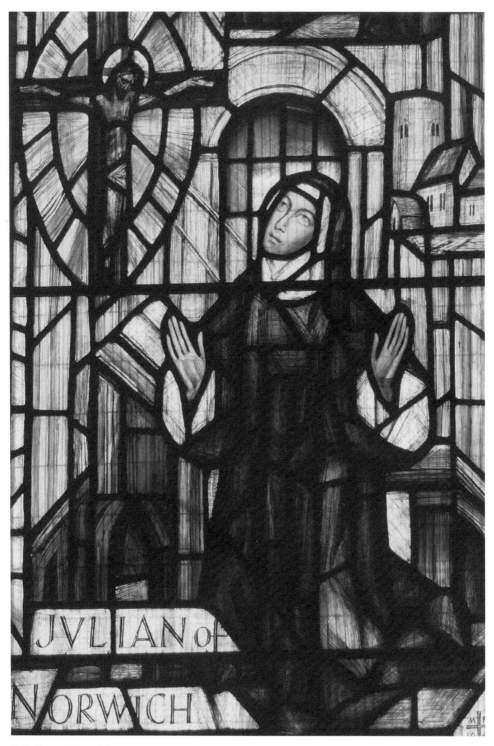

St Julian of Norwich.

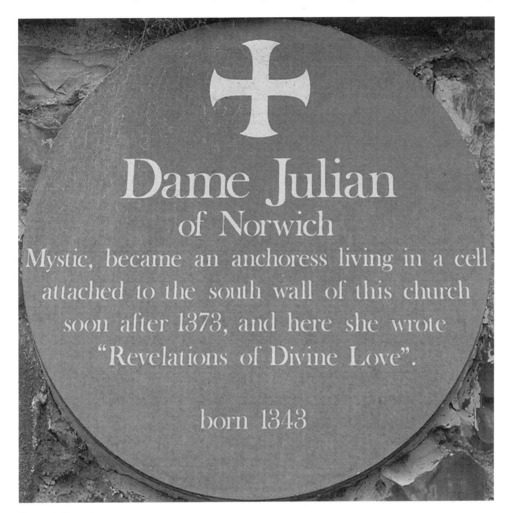

Dame Julian plaque.

Three manuscripts are still said to exist, two in the British Museum and one in the Bibliothèque Nationale, Paris.

Katherine, Anchoress of St Margaret, Newbridge (d. *c.* 1315)

The only information we have about Katherine comes from the Court in Norwich and her will read on Thursday 22 February before the feast of St Peter in Cathedra in Antiochia in the twenty-year reign of Edward II. Katherine's will was brought by the priests Herundun of Happisburgh and Simon of Elingham.

Katherine's messuage in Norwich was to be sold, her debts paid and what was left used to pay for the sake of her soul. The entry of the will was signed by Ervaldi de Stamford.

In 1359 St Margaret's, Newbridge, was reduced to a hermitage chapel in the parish of St George.

Kempe, Margery (1373–1440)

Margery was an English Christian mystic and she dictated *The Book of Margery Kempe*, of which many believed to be the first autobiography written in English. The book is about her own domestic tribulations and her many pilgrims to holy sites across Europe, the holy land and her conversations with God. Margery is today honoured by the Anglican Communion.

Margery was born in Bishop's Lynn, which is now known as King's Lynn. Her Father, John Burnham or Brunham, was a merchant and a Member of Parliament. At the age of twenty Margery married John Kempe and went on to have fourteen children.

Margery was an orthodox Catholic, and like other Catholics she firmly believed that she was being summoned to a 'greater intimacy with Jesus Christ'. After giving birth to her first child, Margery suffered with crises for around eight months and claims to have had many devils and demons attacking her and demanding that she forsake her religion, her family and friends, and ordered her to commit suicide. Margery then claimed that a vision of Christ came to her asking why she had forsaken him. She said she had visitations and begged the vision of Christ for forgiveness and mercy. The vision said that she had been forgiven but gave her a certain amount of commands which were to call him her love, stop wearing the hair shirt, to give up eating meat, to take the Eucharist every Sunday, to pray the rosary only until six o'clock, to be still and to speak to him only in thought, and for the return of this Margery was promised that the vision of Christ would give her victory over her enemies, to answer all clerks and that he would be with her and would never forsake her.

Margery began a life in public of prayer, devotion and tears and at one stage she was imprisoned by the clergy and officials of the town and threatened with the heinous crime of rape. Thankfully this did not take place and Margery dictated her book, which today is known as *The Book of Margery Kempe*, illustrating her visions and life experiences, along with her trial for heresy.

During 1413, Margery visited Julian of Norwich for approval on her visions – which she received – but Julian cautioned her to 'measure these experiences according to the worship they accrue to God and the profit to her fellow Christians'.

The book was completed just before 1450 with the signature of Salthows on the bottom of the last page. The book later became lost and was only kept in the public eye when parts of it were published by Wynkyn de Worde in 1501 and Henry Pepwell in 1521. In 1934 the only surviving manuscript of the book was found by Hope Emily Allen in the private library of the Butler-Bowdon family and has since been published.

During the early 1400s Margery went on a pilgrimage to the Holy Land. She visited Venice and then travelled to Jerusalem via Ramlah. She then went to Bethlehem and then visited Mount Zion, and finally found herself by the River Jordon and Mount Quarentyne. She then stayed in Rome, residing at the Hospital of Saint Thomas of Canterbury until Easter 1415.

In 1417 Margery was back in Norwich for a short time before she set off on a pilgrimage to Santiago de Compostela. She travelled via Bristol residing at Henbury with the Bishop of Worcester, Thomas Prevel. While in Leicester she was arrested by the mayor who, in Latin, accused her of being a 'cheap whore and a lying Lollard'. Also threatened with prison, she insisted that the allegation was made in English and that she be able to defend herself. She was soon cleared, but was then brought to trial by the abbot, dean and mayor, and placed in prison for a period of three weeks before she returning to Lynn in 1418.

Margery is remembered in the Church of England on 9 November and by the Episcopal Church in the USA, together with Richard Rolle and Walter Hilton, on 28 September.

Lambert, Dr Joyce M. (1916–2005)

Doctor Joyce Lambert was a botanist and ecologist who was born in London but was brought up in Brundall. Educated at Norwich High School for Girls, she went on to graduate in botany from University College Wales, Aberystwyth. She started of her working life as a schoolteacher in Norwich, before being appointed a lecturer in botany at Westfield College, London.

Joyce was mentored by Norfolk naturalists A. E. (Ted) Ellis and A. R. Clapman, who advised Dorothy to study the ecology of the fens in

Surlingham during the 1940s. Her findings were published in a series of papers from 1946, and two years later she joined Cambridge University where her subjects gained encouragement from the likes of Harry Godwin and Alfred Steers.

It was up until the early 1950s that the origin of the Broads had been a geographical mystery. Using a small peat borer, Dr Lambert obtained a series of closely spaced cones around the broads. She went on to discover that the lakes had vertical walls and relatively flat bottoms; also, many had steep-sided islands and peninsulas of peat with similar stratigraphy. These profiles and transitions between peat and accumulated mud testified to human activity.

In 1953 Dr Lambert's findings were printed in an article called 'The Past, Present and Future of the Norfolk Broads'. By the mid-1950s Dr Lambert became part of a multidisciplinary team set up to carry out further research, which was backed by Cambridge University along with physiographer J. N. Jennings, historical geographer C. T. Smith, archaeologist C. Green and engineer J. N. Hutchinson. They looked at documents that included the register of St Benet's Abbey, which showed that peat digging had been extensive in the area by the twelfth century.

By the 1950s Joyce was a lecturer in botany at Southampton University. After retiring in 1979, Joyce returned to Norfolk to live in the house that her grandfather built in the 1920s, and she always kept in touch with her beloved Norwich City Football Club.

A Royal Geographical Society memoir called *The Making of the Broads* was published in 1960 and it is now accepted that the broads resulted from peat pits which were excavated in medieval times.

As she was physically incapacitated she spent her last three years in the BUPA nursing home in Colney, but still kept an interest in the Broads. Dr Lambert died on 4 May 2005 of bronchopneumonia.

L'Estrange, Alice (1585–1656)

Lady L'Estrange (*née* Stubbe) was the keeper of the household and estate accounts at Sedgeford Estate and was the only child of Richard and Anne Stubbe. Richard's daughter from his first marriage, Dionsina, was married to Henry Yelverton of Rougham.

Richard was instrumental in the upbringing of Sir Hamon L'Estrange, who was the nephew of Anne Stubbe's first husband, who married Alice on 8 June 1602.

The couple had eight children, with four surviving adulthood. The sons all had works published. Roger was an accomplished pamphleteer, Hamon produced theological works and in contrast to that, Nicholas compiled a book of some forty-three jokes and anecdotes.

Alice harboured some hatred of her half-sister Dionsina. In an account of her father's estate it showed her sister receiving lands worth £498 a year, while Alice's land at Sedgeford was worth £473.

Alice took over the bookkeeping from Hamon in 1609 after the death of their daughter Dorothy, and from 1613 she kept weekly accounts of all the purchases, itemised along with the production and the consumption of food and drink by the household. By 1617 Alice recorded all the profits in her diary.

By 1618 her father was ill and Alice took responsibility for the Sedgeford Estate. She became responsible for receiving rents, but also sheep accounts, grazing times, crop rotations, rentals, field books and organising a survey.

From 1621 Alice kept building accounts for her husband and from 1631 she maintained the entire estates at Hunstanton, Heacham and Ringstead.

While her husband and sons were involved fighting for the King, in the Civil War, Alice did all the work on the estates by herself, including recording their losses and debts. She stopped work in 1654 when her husband died. Alice died two years later at Hunstanton Hall and was buried at Hunstanton church on 9 November 1656.

Lind, Jenny (1820–1887)

Johanna Maria Lind was born on 6 October 1820 in Central Stockholm. The illegitimate child of Niclas Jonas Lind and Anne-Marie Fellborg, she was better known as Jenny Lind, the Swedish Nightingale, and one of the most renowned opera singers of the nineteenth century in Sweden and Europe.

By the early 1840s Jenny suffered vocal damage. Her voice was saved by the teacher Manuel Garcia and she went on to be under great demand to perform, but after two seasons in London she retired from opera at the relatively young age of twenty-nine. By 1840 Carl XIV Johann of Sweden appointed Jenny as his court singer.

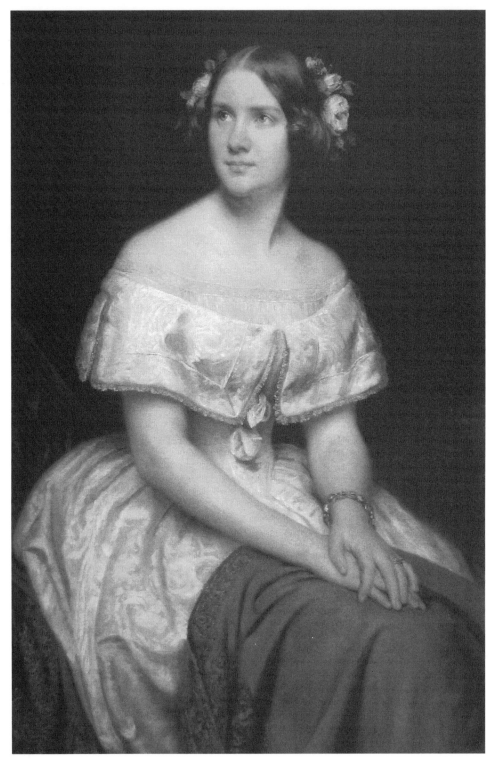

Jenny Lind.

In 1843 Hans Christian Andersen fell in love with Jenny but this was not reciprocated. Instead a good friendship was established, Jenny becoming the inspiration for three of his works: *Beneath the Pillar*, *The Angel* and *The Nightingale*.

Jenny sang as a coloratura soprano with a very wide range, and with regards to her acting she always took on roles that she could identify with, her most famous parts being Alice in *Robert le Diable* by Meyerbeer, Amina in *La Sonnambula* by Bellini, Lucia in *Lucia di Lammermoor* by Donizetti, Maria in *La Fille du Régiment* by Donizetti and Norma in *Norma* by Bellini.

In 1847 Jenny gave her first two concerts in Norwich, proving so popular that a third was soon booked. Jenny went back to Norwich in 1849, staying with Bishop Stanley. She entertained large crowds by giving two concerts in St Andrew's Hall on 22 and 23 January.

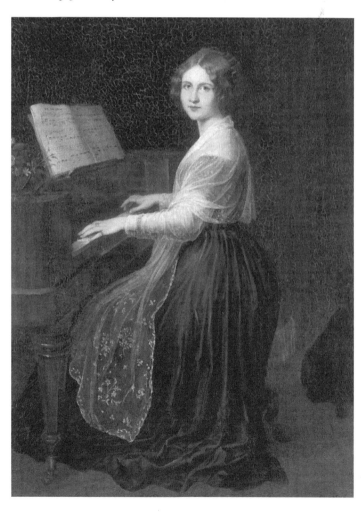

Jenny Lind in later life.

Funds raised from the concerts were put aside to build an infirmary for sick children. A public meeting took place in 1853 endorsing the idea and the hospital opened in 1854 in Pottergate, Norwich.

But by 1850, through the invitation of the legendry P. T. Barnum, Jenny went to America and gave ninety-three concerts, earning an unprecedented $350,000 and donating most of it to charity. Returning to Europe in 1852 with her husband Otto Goldschmidt, she gave birth to three children and gave few concerts. She later settled in England where she took up the position of professor of singing at the Royal College of Music in London. Jenny died on 2 November 1887.

Under her married name of Jenny Lind Goldschmidt she is commemorated in Poet's Corner in Westminster Abbey, and there is, of course, the Jenny

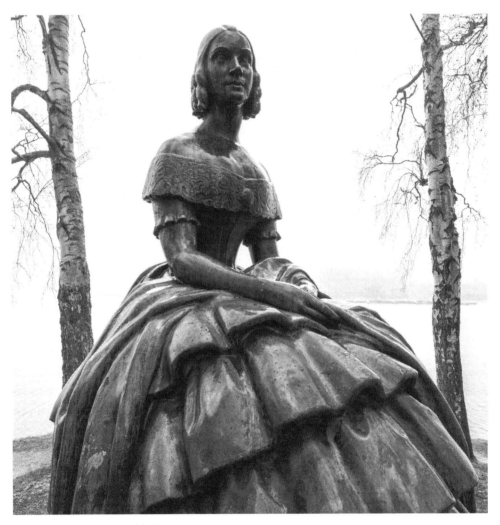

Jenny Lind statue in Stockholm.

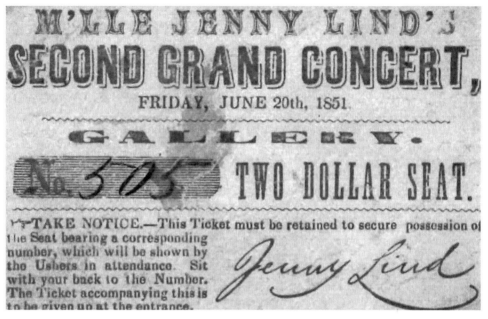

Jenny Lind concert.

Lind Children's Hospital in Norfolk and Norwich University Hospital. There are plaques at the two London addresses where she lived – at The Boltons, Kensington, and at No. 189 Old Brompton Road. In 1996 and 2006 the Swedish fifty-krona banknote had her portrait on the front. In 1930 the Hollywood film *A Lady's Morals* starred Grace Moore as Jenny. In 2001 the film *Hans Christian Andersen: My Life as a Fairytale* featured Flora Montgomery as Jenny, and in 2005 the musician Elvis Costello said that he was writing an opera about Jenny Lind.

Mann, Mary (1848–1929)

Mary E. Mann (*née* Rackham) was born in Norwich on 14 August 1848 to a Norwich merchant named William Simon Rackham. She was married to Fairman Joseph Mann and the couple moved to Shropham where Fairman was a farmer, church warden and parish guardian. Mary was involved with the Union Workhouse, visiting the sick often.

It was an in-law, Thomas Fairman Ordish, who guided Mary towards writing in the 1880s. Her first novel was *The Parish of Hilby* (1883). Her writing career lasted thirty-five years and she published forty books overall which were based on Norfolk yeoman farmers.

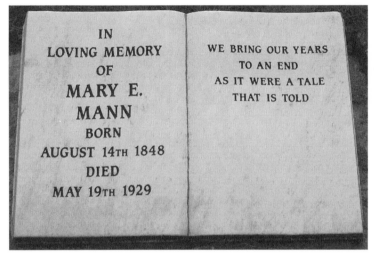

Mary Mann's grave.

Dulditch was the name given to Shropham in her novels. Mary went on to be known as Norfolk's Thomas Hardy and was greatly admired by D. H. Lawrence.

Fairman died in 1913 and Mary moved to Sheringham where she died aged eighty. She is buried in Shropham churchyard and her epitaph is a follows:

We Bring Our Years
To an End
As it were a Tale
That is Told

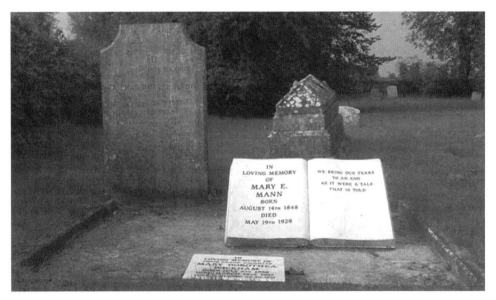

Mary Mann's graveside.

Marshall, Emma (Miss Martin) (1829–1899)

Emma was born in 1830 to Simon Martin, who was a partner in Gurney's Norwich bank, and Hannah, at Northrepps Hill House in Cromer. The family soon settled in Norwich, where Emma received a private education until she was sixteen.

In 1849 Emma and her mother went to live in Bristol where a friendship with Dr Addington Symonds gave them an insight into the society of the area. It was here that Emma began to write, and her first book, *Happy Days at Fernbank*, was published in 1861. Emma would think of an historical character, landmark or building and write the book around them. She would go on to have over 200 novels published.

In 1854 Emma married Hugh Graham Marshall who was employed by the West of England Bank. During their marriage the couple resided at Wells, Exeter, Gloucester and Longfellow. Their youngest daughter, Christabel, also became a writer and a campaigner for women's suffrage.

In 1879 the West of England Bank went bankrupt, leaving Hugh without a position or a wage, but as a shareholder he had certain legal liabilities and Emma cleared all debts through her writing.

Mary died from pneumonia at her home in Clifton on 4 May 1899 and is buried in Long Ashton Cemetery. Her last book, *The Parson's Daughter*, was completed by her daughter Beatrice.

Martin, Sarah (1791–1843)

Sarah Martin, a philanthropist and a prison visitor, was born in 1791 at Caister, just outside of Great Yarmouth. Both her parents died when she was a child and she was raised by her grandmother. School education was very limited. She was later sent to Great Yarmouth to learn dressmaking at 1 shilling per day.

Sarah's life was changed when in 1819 a woman was sent to Yarmouth Gaol for assaulting and ill-using her own child. Sarah was twenty-eight at the time and the crime made it into many newspapers, making Sarah want to visit the prison and read the Bible to the inmates. Sarah knocked on the jail door asking to see the prisoner of whom she had read about. The keep, in no uncertain terms, said no. This did not stop Sarah and at the second attempt she was admitted.

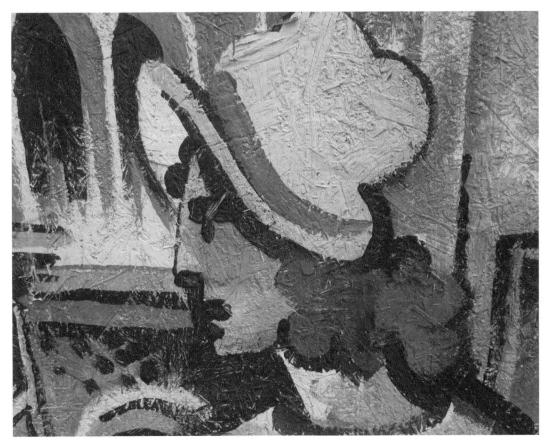

Sarah Martin, King Street, Great Yarmouth.

The guilty mother stood before Sarah and told her that she needed to know of her guilt and of God's mercy. On hearing this the woman broke down, cried and thanked her.

Sarah is later quoted to have said that since the year 1810, and before Elizabeth Fry visited Newgate, she had a strong desire to visit the inmates at Yarmouth Gaol to read the Bible to them. She continued visiting along with other prisons, helping the inmates with their reading and writing. Doing this one day a week meant her earnings were cut and she went on to say, 'To give up a day in the week from dressmaking to serve the prisoners. This, regularly given, with many an additional one, was not felt as a pecuniary loss, but was ever followed with abundant satisfaction for the blessing of God was upon me.'

Sarah later went on to form a Sunday service, and then introduced benefits to prisoners. In 1823 she accepted donations from two gentlemen for the sum of

10 shillings each for prison charity. With the money Sarah purchased materials to make clothes for babies and set the female prisoners to work. Money was divided and given to the prisoners on their release. For the men, she taught them how to make straw hats, caps, shirts and patchworks. A fund was set up by Sarah out of the prisoners earnings so that they would have further funds after release.

Sarah's grandmother died in 1826 and left her around £12. This enabled her to take two rooms in Yarmouth. One lady in Yarmouth allowed Sarah a rest from sewing one day a week by paying her the same if she had been working. All of her free time was now spent with prisoners.

In the second report of the Inspector of Prisons 1836, Captain William's account stated,

Sunday, November 28, 1835. – Attended divine service in the morning at the prison. The male prisoners only were assembled. A female resident in the town officiated; her voice was exceedingly melodious, her delivery emphatic, and her enunciation distinct. The service was the Liturgy of the Church of England; two psalms were sung by the whole of the prisoners, and extremely well, – much better than I have frequently heard in our best-appointed churches. A written discourse, of her own composition, was read by her; it was of a purely moral tendency ... involving no doctrinal points, and admirably suited to the hearers. During the performance of the service, the prisoners said the profoundest attention and the most marked respect; and as far as it was possible to judge, appeared to take a devout interest. Evening service was read by her, afterwards, to the female prisoners.

As well as helping the prisoners, Sarah spent the evenings at the workhouse where she looked after the school. In the evenings Sarah would return to her own poverty-stricken abode, but she did not care for herself.

As age set upon her, Yarmouth borough saw the good work that Sarah was doing and awarded her a salary of £12 a year. She decided to refuse the offer, as hers had been a labour of love throughout. What is disturbing about this is that Sarah gave her life to the prison and the prisoners and the jail committee returned the thanks by stating the following: 'If we permit you to visit the prison, you must submit to our terms.' She was then paid the salary of £12 for her role of jail chaplain and schoolmaster.

Sarah's health began to suffer in 1842, but she still kept up her daily visits to the prison. By 17 April 1843 however, Sarah had become disabled and had to stop. She took to her bed and stated to a close friend,

> I seem to lie
> So near the heavenly portals bright,
> I catch the streaming rays that fly
> From eternity's own light.

Sarah died on 15 October 1843 and was buried at Caister with an inscription that she wrote herself:

> Only the actions of the just
> Smell sweet, and blossom in the dust.

On the following Sunday after her death, a sermon composed by herself was preached at Yarmouth Gaol, and Bishop Stanley of Norwich declared, 'I would canonise Sarah Martin if I could!'

Martineau, Harriet (1802–1876)

Harriet was born in Norwich in 1802 to textile manufacturer Thomas and his wife Elizabeth. Harriet became deaf at the age of twelve and used an aid for the rest of her life. The family were Unitarians and in all there were four sons and four daughters. The family believed in education but also expected the girls to stay at home once their education had finished.

Harriet was firmly against this and in 1823 she had published anonymously an article regarding the details on female education in the Unitarian journal, the *Monthly Repository*. It was praised by her brother and she decided to make a living as a writer.

She became engaged to John Hugh Worthington. The relationship had lots of problems and it came to an end when John became ill and died.

Harriet continued to write for the *Monthly Repository*, but when her father died in 1826 she knew that she would have to support herself with needlework jobs until her writing began to pay off.

After the success of her book *Illustrations of Political Economy*, Harriet moved to London in 1832 where she classed Hallam, Milman, Malthus,

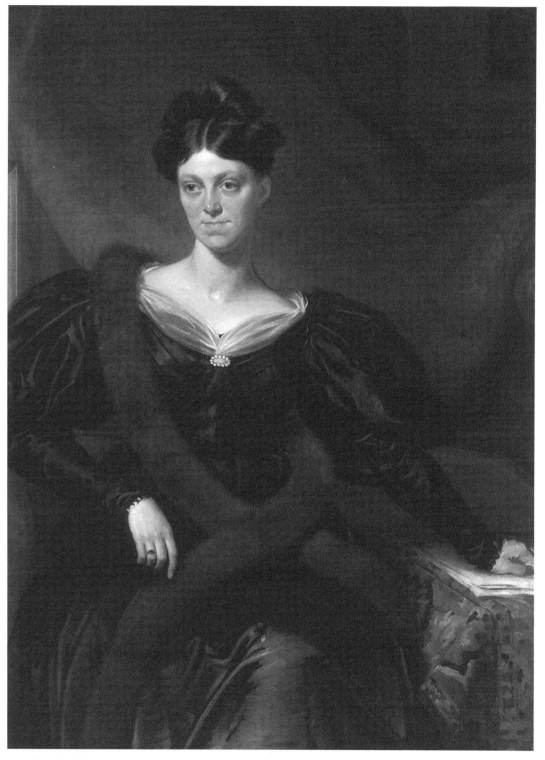

Harriet Martineau.

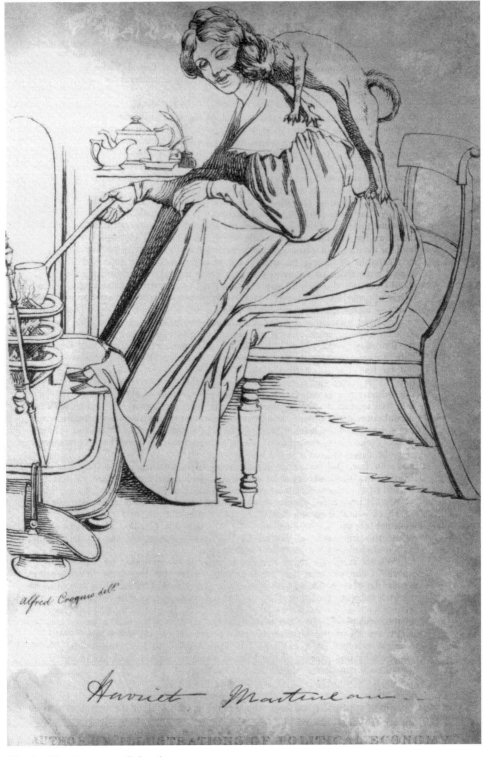

Harriet Martineau pencil sketch.

Monckton Milnes, Sydney Smith and Bulwer among her friends. She became very successful and spent two years travelling America where she became drawn to the anti-slavery cause. She returned to England in 1837 and published *Society in America*. Her first novel, *Deerbrook*, was published in 1839 and she soon became prolific. She published *The Hour and the Man*, which was about Toussaint L'Ouverture, the Haitian leader. She even turned her skills to writing for children in 1841.

While travelling in Europe, Harriet became ill and was brought back to Newcastle to be treated by her brother-in-law Thomas Michael Greenhow. She took to renting a property in Tynemouth and it was here that she suffered from a prolapsed uterus. It was here also that she believed she was cured by mesmerism and after five years she went back to work.

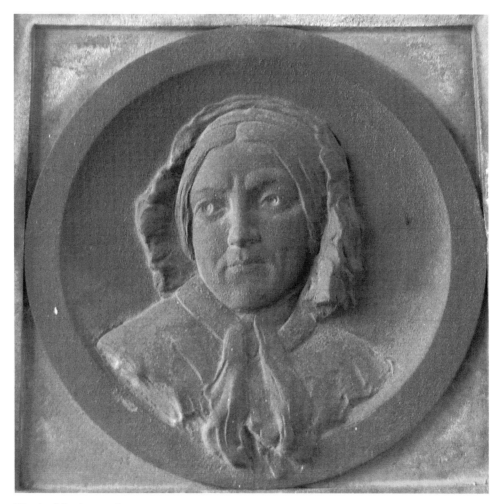

Harriet Martineau plaque.

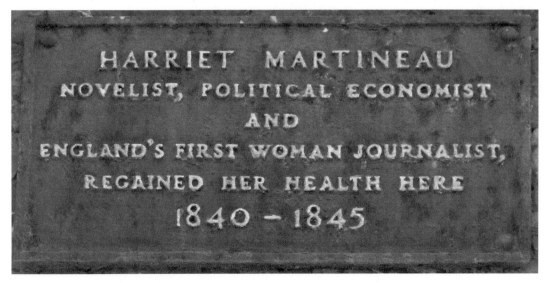

Harriet Martineau plaque.

Moving to the Lake District in 1845, she built a house at Ambleside and continued to be a prolific writer. Joining the staff of the *Daily News* in 1852, she spent sixteen years writing over 1,500 articles, including articles about women in employment for the *Edinburgh Review*. In 1866, along with others, she signed a petition to Parliament to allow women the vote.

Even after she retired, Harriet kept on writing, including articles for *the Daily News* attacking the Contagious Diseases Act introduced to reduce venereal disease in the armed forces. She also helped to form the National Association for the Repeal of the Contagious Diseases Acts.

In 1855, Harriet had written her two-volume autobiography, which was only published after her death at Ambleside in 1876, and which came with a third volume of commentary by her American abolitionist friend Mary Weston Chapman.

Meynell, Alicia (b. 1782)

Alicia Meynell was born in 1782 to a watchmaker from Norwich. She went on to gain a love of horse riding and hounds and she owned three hunters. She would go riding with her brother-in-law William Flint of Yorkshire and on one occasion they discussed whose horse was the best.

They decided to race together and twice Alicia won, prompting William to challenge Alicia to a real race at Newmarket for a prize to the tune of 1,000 guineas. Alicia accepted and news spread to those wanting to see a woman

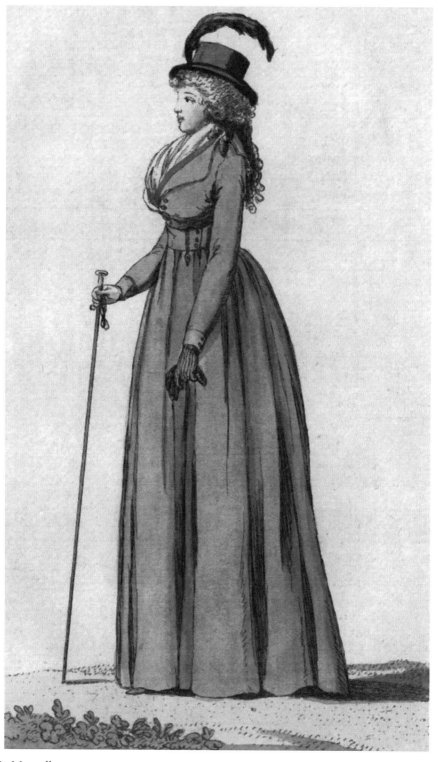

Alicia Meynell.

race for the first time. So enormous was the crowd that the 6th Light Dragoons were called in to keep order. Those watching had placed bets up to £200.

When the race started Alicia went into the lead, but William soon drew level before pulling ahead and finally winning the race. Alicia took losing very badly, while the crowd heaped praise on William for racing with a woman. Alicia wrote to the *Herald* to slate William and to request a rematch, but no reply was given, and this could have been because Alicia's lover, Lieutenant-Colonel Thomas Thornton, refused to honour the bet, claiming that it had all been a joke.

A Mr Bromford then asked Alicia to take place in next year's race for a prize of £2,000 and bottles of French wine. The race never took place as Bromford left, meaning that Alicia won the race by default. Alicia was given a chance to ride against Buckle, the highest-paid jockey of the time. Alicia rode a mare called Louisa and won by half a neck. William was at the event and on seeing Thornton he horsewhipped him and was confined for assault. The two men spent years in court over the matter, which Thornton went on to win.

In 1806 Alicia ran off with a soldier and she went on to be the only woman listed in the records of England's Jockey Club to have raced and won against a man until 1943.

Nichols, Sarah Anne

Sarah Anne Nichols was a ladies' maid who kept a diary, now housed at the Norfolk Record Office. She travelled with Anna Gurney, Sarah Buxton and Miss Carr.

Opie, Amelia (1771–1853)

Amelia Opie (*née* Alderson) was born on 12 November 1769 to physician James Alderson and Amelia Briggs of Norwich. Amelia became an author, writing about the Romantic period, and was also a leading abolitionist in Norwich.

As a youngster, Amelia was high spirited and she sang ballads of her own composition and gave recitations. Aged eighteen, she wrote a tragedy called *Adelaide* which she acted for her friends, playing the title role herself.

She enjoyed visiting the Norwich Assizes and soon found herself listening to trials of treason such as Horne Tooke and Holycroft at the Old Bailey. When Horne Tooke was acquitted she walked up to him and kissed him.

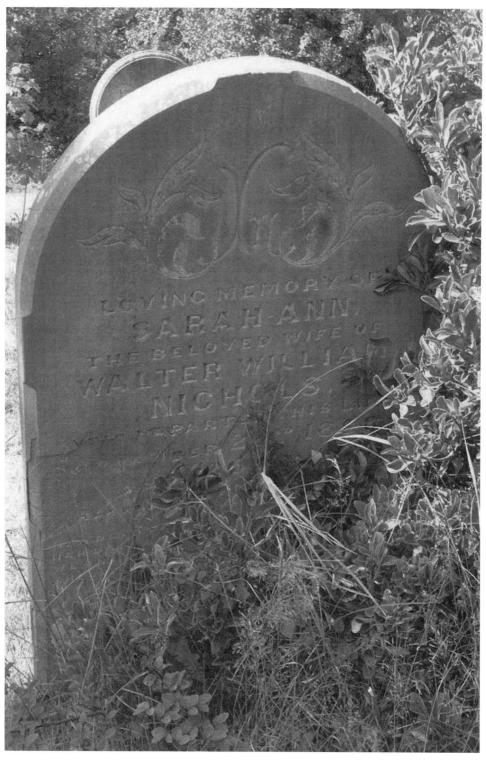

Sarah Ann Nichols grave.

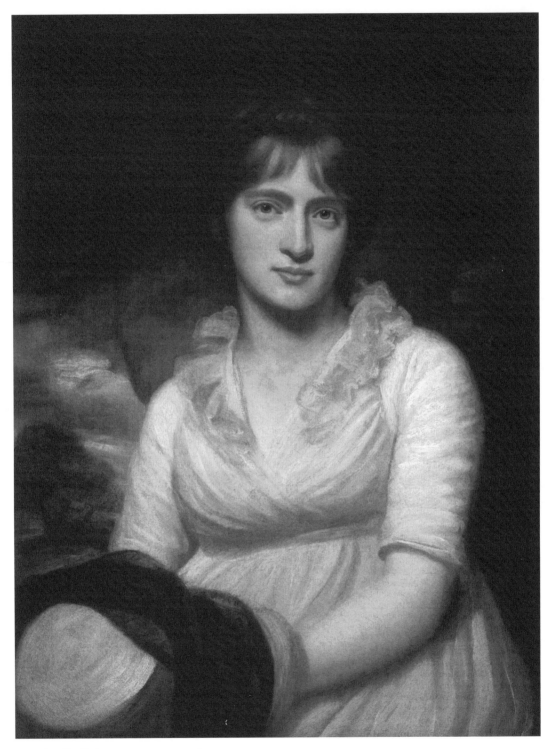

Amelia Opie.

At a dinner party in London in 1797 she met the divorced painter John Opie and in 1798 they married at Marylebone church, London. John Opie did not share her love of society, although in 1801 he did encourage her to complete the novel *Father and Daughter* and a year after that she had published a volume of verse. She continued writing and divided her time between London and Norwich. She kept friendships with Walter Scott, Richard Brinsley Sheridan and Madam de Stael.

John died on 9 April 1807 and Amelia returned to Norwich to live with her father. She joined the Quakers and ceased novel writing. Her last novel, *Madeline*, was published in two volumes in 1822. She did start another novel but this remained unfinished.

Amelia wrote a letter to Elizabeth Fry on 6 of December 1823 stating:

> As it is possible that thou mayest have been told that a new novel from my pen called 'The Painter and his Wife' is in the press, I wish to tell thee this is a falsehood; that my publishers advertised this only began work unknown to me, and that I have written to say the said work is not written, nor ever will be. I must own to thee, however, that as several hundreds of it are already ordered by the trade, I have felt the sacrifice, but I do not repent of it.

Amelia's father died in 1825 and under the guidance of Joseph John Gurney she joined the Society of Friends, something her father was opposed to. She spent many years travelling and doing charity work, such as helping out in workhouses, hospitals, prisons and helping the poor. She went on with Anna Gurney to form the Ladies Anti-Slavery Society in Norwich.

Amelia became ill in 1834 but still found time to visit the Highlands in Scotland. She then travelled to Belgium, Germany and Switzerland before settling back in Norwich. In 1840 she attended the Anti-Slavery Convention in London as delegate for Norwich.

In 1848 Amelia purchased a house on Castle Meadow, Norwich; the street is now called Opie Street. She continued to attend the Assizes and in 1851 she visited the Great Exhibition in a wheelchair, aged eighty-two.

After catching a chill while in Cromer, Amelia took to her bed. At midnight on 2 December 1853, she died at Norwich and is buried at the Gildencroft Quaker Cemetery here.

All of her writings were intended to point to certain morals.

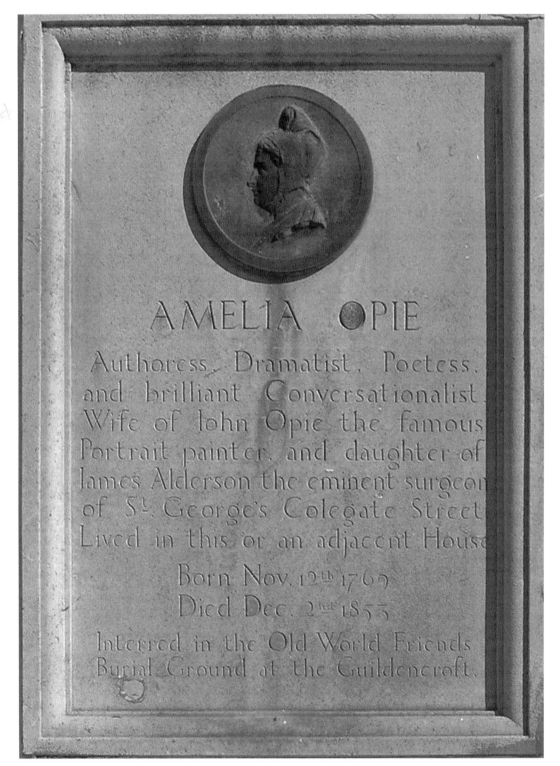

Amelia Opie house plaque.

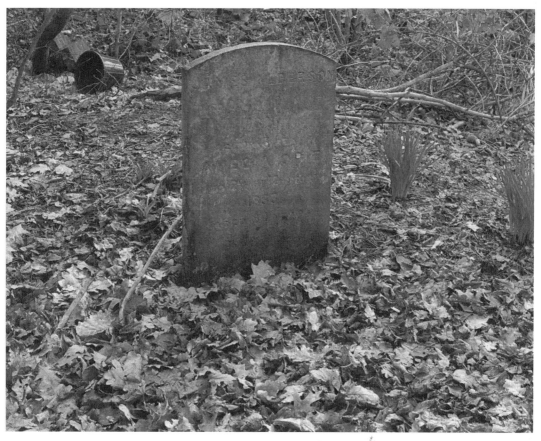

Amelia Opie's grave.

Pallis, Marietta (1882–1963)

Marietta was born in Bombay in 1882 to Greek poet Alexandros Pallis; her younger brother was the author Marco Pallis. The family came to England in 1894, settling in Liverpool where Marietta studied botany at the university before attending Newnham College, Cambridge. Later she resided at Long Gores Farm, a marshland property in Hickling.

She studied aquatic vegetation in the river valleys of East Norfolk and she started to write about the floating reed systems of the Danube Delta for the Linnaean Society With her partner, Phyllis Clark, she travelled the eastern Mediterranean.

Back at Long Gores Marietta, started to plant seeds that she brought back from her travels and also created a devotional symbolic Greek landscape which featured a Double-Headed eagle pool – a pool with an island, designed to be in the shape of a crowned, double-headed Byzantine eagle featuring the Papal Cross and her Greek initials.

In 1939 she published *General Aspects of the Vegetation of Europe*. She wrote about Greek history and culture in many pamphlets during the 1950s and 1960s, which she called 'philosophical biology', as well as continuing her research in aquatic botany, concentrating on the Danube Delta and the Norfolk Broads.

Marietta died in Norwich in 1963 aged eighty-one. She is buried with partner Phyllis Clark near the Norfolk Broads on the central island of the Double-Headed Eagle Pool. The tree *Fraxinus Pallisia* is named after her.

Before she died she published information on the permeability of peat and the status of the Ferns. Her plants are housed at Kew.

Paston, Margaret (1421–1484)

Born into a great family of Norfolk in 1423, Margaret's marriage in 1441 to John Paston, son of William and Agnes, was an extremely happy union, even though it was arranged. Margaret would look after her husband's portfolio of properties while he was away. The family lived at No. 20 Elm Hill, where the Strangers Club now stands. However, in recent years it has been disputed that the family home was situated at Nos 41 to 43, but the houses would have been destroyed in the fire of 1507. The couple had seven children.

The Paston family were prolific in their correspondence to each other from the years 1422 to 1509 and this is something they are now renowned for. They were first published in the eighteenth century and Margaret was the writer of 104 items. Letters show that Margaret and John moved to a property near St Peter Hungate and in 1458 they paid for the rebuilding of the nave and transepts to the church. The couple also financed repairs to St Andrew's and Blackfriars Hall; they also purchased property in King Street. Their son, Sir John Paston, bought the Music House in King Street which was once owned by Jurnet the Jew in the times of Henry II. The property still stands today, forming part of Wensum Education. The Paston Letters are housed in the British Museum, although a few are housed in the Norfolk Record Office.

Margaret died in 1484 aged sixty-one, eighteen years after the death of her husband, and is buried at Mautby.

PROVISIONS FOR LENT

To my right worshipful husband, John Paston, be this delivered in haste

Right worshipful husband, I recommend me to you, beseeching you that ye be not displeased with me, through my simpleness caused you for me to be displeased with me; by my truth it is not my will neither to do nor say that should cause you for to be displeased, and if I have done, I am sorry thereof, and will amend it; Wherefore I beseech you to forgive me, and that ye bear none heaviness in your heart against me, for displeasure should be too heavy to me to endure with.

I send you the Roll that ye sent for, ensealed by the bringer hereof; it was found in your trussing Coffer. As for Herring, I have bought a horse-load for 4s. and 6d. I can get no Eels yet; as for Bever [a light drink] there is promised me some, but I might not get it you. I sent to Joan Petche to have an answer for the windows, for she might not come to me; and she sent me word that she had spoken thereof to Thomas Ingham, and he said that he should speak with you himself, and he should accord with you well enough, and said to her it was not her part to desire of him to stop the lights; and also he said it was not his part to do it, because the place is his but for years.

And as for other errands that ye have commanded for to be done, they shall be done as soon as they may be done. The blessed Trinity have you in his keeping.

Written at Norwich, on the Monday after next Saint Edward.

Yours

MARGARET PASTON

A PROPOSAL OF MARRIAGE

To my right worshipful Husband John Paston, be this letter delivered I haste.

Right worshipful Husband, I recommend me to you, please you to weet that I was at Norwich this week to purvey such things as needeth me against this winter; and I was at my Mother's, and whilst I was there, there came in one Wrothe, a kinsman of Elizabeth Clere's and he saw your daughter and praised her to my Mother, and said that she was a goodly young woman; and my Mother prayed him for to get her one good marriage if he knew any; and he said he knew one should be of a 300 marks [£200] by year, the which is Sir John Cley's son, that is Chamberlayn with my Lady of York, and he is of age of 18 years old; if ye think it be far to spoken of, my Mother thinks that it should be got for less money now in this world than it should be hereafter, either that one, or some other good marriage …

As far answer [of] other matters, Daubeney [Paston's agent] telleth me he wrote to you. I beseech Almighty God have you in his keeping.

Written at Caister, the Sunday next after Saint Martin.

By your
MARGARET PASTON

Pilling, Mary (c. 1929)

Mary Pilling (*née* Woodrow) from Withington, Lancashire, purchased the land in Norwich off Harvey Lane for £2,000 and gave it as a gift to Norwich City Council in memory of her father Jeremiah Woodrow, who had moved away from Norwich in 1829 but loved and missed the city. It was named the Jeremiah Woodrow Recreation Ground and it opened in 1929.

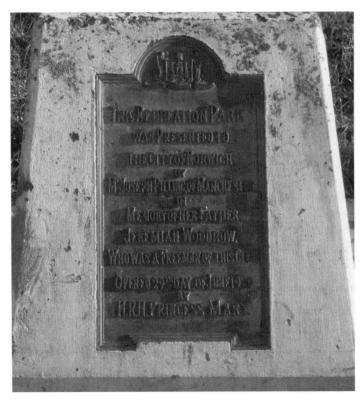

Mary Pilling park plaque.

Reeve, Lucilla Maud (1889–1950)

Lucilla was born in Hunstanton in 1889. Her father was not known, although some have suggested that he may have been Lord Walsingham. She was brought up in Tottington by her grandparents, who came from a long line of agricultural labourers. Her education in London was paid anonymously.

Just before the outbreak of the First World War Lucilla took up the position of Land Agent on the Merton Estate in Breckland for Lord Walsingham.

Just before the start of the Second World War, when farming was at a low, Lucilla took on the tenancy of Bagmore Farm, Stanford, and made it a success. By the 1930s she had given her support to the National Socialist Movement and had been pictured with Oswald Mosely. In 1940 her house was surrounded by the military and she was arrested for a day.

Lucilla was patriotic and produced food for the nation, and she was a member of Wayland Rural District Council. In 1941 the War Agricultural Executive Committee stated that the army needed the area for training, which meant that 150 houses and thirty farms had to be vacated. Lucilla moved to what was known as the battle area, which consisted of duck sheds, a bedroom, a kitchen and office, although it came to an abrupt halt in 1942 when the army took over the area for tank training. While there she wrote the book *The Earth No Longer Bare* with all profits being given to the St Dunstan's Institution for the Blind.

By the end of 1942 she purchased Broadmarsh Farm in Great Ellingham. After the war people who once lived in the battle area were told that they could never return. In 1950 they were offered compensation but at 1938 prices.

Lucilla suffered with depression and spent time in hospital at Thorpe St Andrew. On Remembrance Day in 1950 she was found hanging in a barn. She is buried at Tottington.

Rigby, Elizabeth (Lady Eastlake) (1809–1893)

Lady Elizabeth Eastlake (*née* Rigby) was born on 17 November 1809 to classical scholar and Dr Edward Rigby and his wife Anne.

Elizabeth had a long-lasting love of art, and although privately educated she studied art into her middle twenties. In 1827 she became very ill and was sent to Germany and Switzerland to recover and stayed for two years. It was Switzerland where she started translating Passavant's essay on English art, which lasted until her death. She also wrote articles when in Germany for Goethe and went on to visit a sister in Estonia. In 1841 she published a book on her letters and travels called *A Residence on the Shores of the Baltic* and later was invited by the editor of *Quarterly Review*, J. G. Lockhart, to write for him.

After her father died, her mother Anne moved to be with her daughter in Edinburgh, where Elizabeth was working on an essay showing the relationship between art and photography.

In 1846 Elizabeth married Sir Charles Eastlake and together they enjoyed a healthy social life entertaining the artists of the day. During the 1850s and 1860s the couple visited many European countries in search for new art for a gallery.

Sir Charles died in 1865 and Elizabeth continued to write about art and artists until she died on 2 October 1893. Her close friends included Sir Robert Peel and the Duke of Wellington. She was buried at Kensal Green, near her husband, for whom, knowing his wishes, she had declined a funeral in St Paul's.

Elizabeth will always be remembered for her scathing review of *Jane Eyre*, which she disliked.

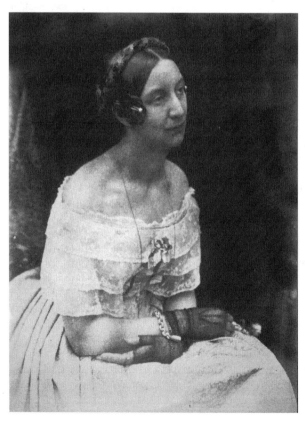

Elizabeth Rigby (Lady Eastlake).

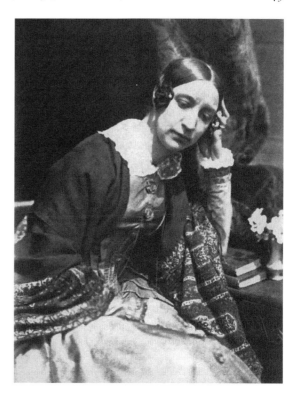

Elizabeth Rigby (Lady Eastlake).

Robsart, Amy (1532–1560)

Amy Robsart was born in Norfolk to Sir John Robsart of Syderstone and his wife Elizabeth Scott. Amy grew up as a Protestant at her mother's house, Stanfield Hall. Three days before her eighteenth birthday, Amy married Robert Dudley, who was the youngest son of John Dudley, Earl of Warwick. The wedding contract that was signed in May 1550 stated that Amy would inherit her father's estate only after the death of both parents, which meant that both Amy and Robert would rely financially on their fathers.

The marriage took place on 4 June 1550 at the Royal Palace of Sheen, with guests including Edward VI.

The Earl of Warwick, who would go on to be the Duke of Northumberland, was the most powerful man in England, and with his son marrying Amy, it went on to strengthen his control in Norfolk. The couple divided their time by spending six months with her parents and then six months with his.

On her marriage to Guildford Dudley, Robert's brother, Lady Jane Grey became Amy's sister-in-law in 1553. For his involvement in the plan to put Jane on the throne, Robert was sentenced to death and sent to the Tower

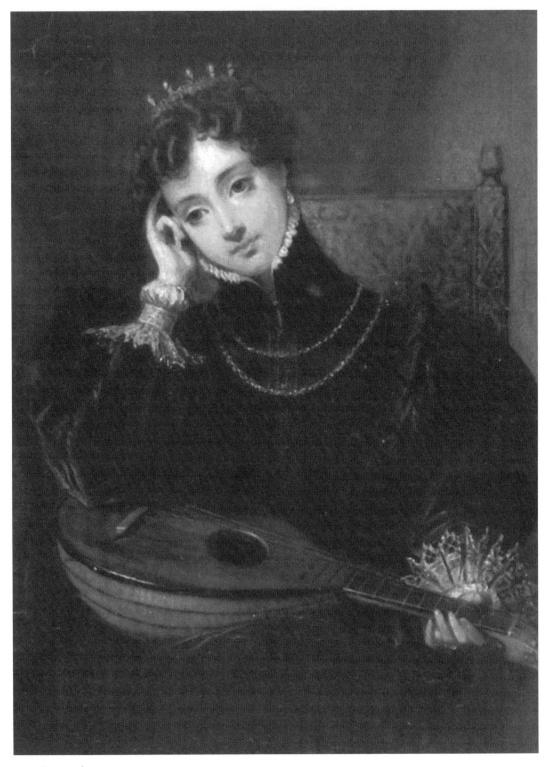

Amy Robsart.

of London, staying there from July 1553 until October 1554. When he was
released both he and Amy remained reliant on their families for all things
financial. Sir John Robsart died in 1554 and his wife died in 1557. This
meant that Amy and Robert could inherit the Robsart estate with royal
permission. The manor house of Syderstone had been left unattended for
many years and the couple moved to Throcking in Hertfordshire.

In August 1577 Robert went to fight for King Consort Philip II at the Battle
of St Quentin in France. A year later Amy and Robert tirelessly searched for
a property in Norfolk, but nothing was found. Mary I died in November
1558 and when her sister Elizabeth I took to the throne, Robert became her
Master of the Horse. It was soon clear to all those at court that Elizabeth and
Robert had fallen in love. At this point, Amy became ill with possible breast
cancer. During the latter part of 1559 Amy was residing at Compton Verney
in Warwickshire, the home of Sir Richard Verney and the Spanish Ambassador
de Quadra and his staff claimed that Robert was sending Amy poison. Many
peers complained that Robert's influence at court was stopping the queen from
marrying and there were many plots to assassinate him. The last time Amy and
Robert met was in London in the 1559. Amy was now living at Cumnor Place,
Abingdon, then in Berkshire, but now part of Oxfordshire. The rent was paid
direct from her father's estate and Amy had ten servants.

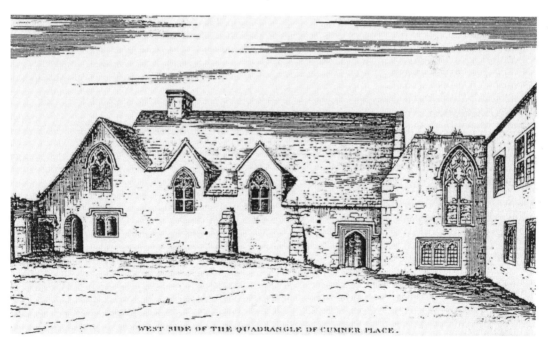

WEST SIDE OF THE QUADRANGLE OF CUMNER PLACE.

Amy Robsart's home.

On Sunday 8 September 1560 Amy was found dead at the foot of a staircase at Cumnor Place. Robert was told of her death the next day while staying with the queen at Windsor Castle. Robert sent his steward Thomas Blount to see what had happened. Blount asked Amy's maid Mrs Picto whether she believed what had happened was 'chance or villany' and her reply was that by her faith she doth judge very chance, and neither done by man nor by herself.

The coroner and the fifteen local men who made up the jury at the local Assizes on 1 August 1561 pronounced that Lady Dudley, being alone in a certain chamber, accidently fell precipitously down the adjoining stairs to the very bottom of the same where she sustained two head injuries.

Anne was buried at St Mary's, Oxford, and Robert, as was custom, did not attend but did pay the sum of £2,000 for the burial. Robert then spent six

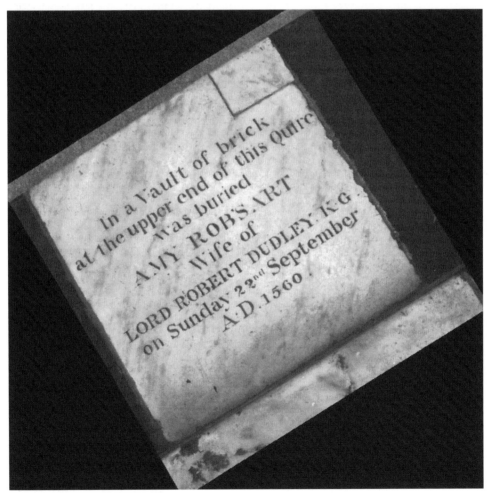

Amy Robsart vault.

months in mourning at his home in Kew while the court spent over a month in mourning.

Shortly after the burial, rumours started to appear about Robert's intentions with Elizabeth; in fact, the Queen's Principal Secretary, William Cecil, felt threatened by this and started to spread his own rumours. He spoke to the Spanish Ambassador saying that Lord Robert and the queen wished to marry and that they were about to poison Lady Dudley.

The English Ambassador in France, Nicholas Throckmorton, drew his attention to what was being said at the French court. Both Nicholas and Cecil used what they heard to their own gains, even though they did not believe that Robert had had his wife killed. When Robert returned to court he knew that his reputation had been ruined.

The first written works of Amy's death appeared in the satirical libel *Leicester's Commonwealth*, which was in opposition of the Earl of Leicester and written by Catholic exiles in 1584. It states that Sir Richard Verney went to Cumnor Place and ordered the servants to go to the market. He then breaks Amy's neck and places her by the foot of the stairs. The jury's verdict is murder.

In the nineteenth century Amy's story became popularised by the Walter Scott novel *Kenilworth* – strangely enough, the villain of the peace is called Verney. James Froude, a Victorian historian, was convinced of Leicester's role in what had happened, and in 1863 he stated that Amy was murdered by her husband, and Dudley had used private means to prevent the search from being pressed inconveniently far.

Walter Rye's book *The Murder of Amy Robsart* (1885) claimed that Amy was at first poisoned and killed by violent means. By 1910 A. F. Pollard stated that Amy's death caused so much suspicion that it would have made marriage between Elizabeth I and Lord Robert Dudley impossible.

What is incredible about this case is that the coroner's report only came to light in 2008 at the National Archives, and what happened to Amy could have been an accident, suicide or a form of violence. In 1956, professor of medicine Ian Aird stated that Amy could have been suffering from breast cancer, which was known, and that metastatic cancerous deposits in the spine might have caused Amy's neck to break under little strain.

Numerous claims over hundreds of years state that there was a possibility that Amy committed suicide because of illness, depression and being separated from Robert. The view of Sir Richard Verney killing Amy after alleged failed attempts to poison her were claimed by George Bernard and Chris Skidmore in the *Chronicles of John Hales*, published in 1563, and the 1584 libel *Leicester's Commonwealth*.

Claims that the jury could have been influenced by Robert have been argued along with the point that the jury foreman, Sir Richard Smith, had previously been a household servant of Princess Elizabeth and was known for his loyalty. It was also stated that Robert gave a certain Mr Smith, also known for his loyalty to the queen, a present. Is it possible that Sir Richard Smith and Mr Smith were the same?

Sewell, Anna (1820–1878)

Anna Sewell was born on 30 March 1820 in Great Yarmouth to a Quaker family. Her father was Phillip Sewell and her mother was children's author Mary Wright Sewell. Along with her younger brother Phillip, Anna was mainly educated at home. Her birth home has been a museum and is now a tea shop.

The family soon moved to London, but her father suffered financial trouble and in 1832 the family moved to Stoke Newington in London. While walking home one day, Anna slipped and fell over injuring both her ankles, which would cause her problems standing for the rest of her life.

Her father moved the family to Brighton with the view that the climate would help Anna with her disability. This was not to be and Anna would spend the rest of her life using a crutch and horse-drawn carriages.

Anna travelled all over Europe hoping to cure her health, and started to mix with writers and artists. It was on one of these trips that she met the poet Lord Alfred Tennyson. When back in England, Anna settled into a house in Old Catton just outside of Norwich, and it was at this home between the years 1871 to 1877 that Anna wrote her only novel, *Black Beauty*. She became very ill during this time, confining herself to bed, finding writing a challenge. The text was dictated to her mother, and by 1876 Anna began to write on scraps of paper that her mother transcribed. *Black Beauty* was sold to Norwich publisher Jarrolds on 24 November 1877.

The main outcome of the book was Anna's constant message of compassion and understanding, which in some cases saw the abolishment of bearing or check reins being used on carriage horses (reins which forced horses to carry their head at a harsh angle).

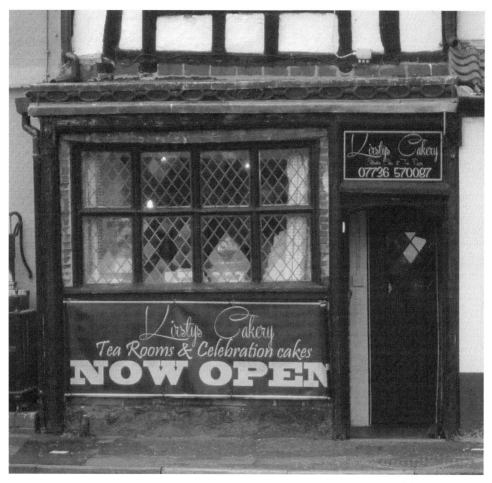

Anna Sewell's birthplace.

Anna died from tuberculosis on 25 April 1878, five months after *Black Beauty* was published, and is buried in the Quaker burial grounds at Lammas, Buxton.

Phyllis Briggs wrote a sequel called *Son of Beauty* in 1950 and *Black Beauty* itself has been adapted into film and television shows. In 1996 Spike Milligan wrote a parody called *Black Beauty According to Spike Milligan*. In 2011 *Black Beauty Live* was performed at the Broughton Hall Estate, North Yorkshire, and Epson Racecourse, Surrey – a critical success which went on to be performed around the UK in 2012.

In Sewell Park, Norwich, is a commemorative horse trough in honour of Anna. Black Beauty was based on her brother's horse Bessie, and Merrylegs was based on Anna's own little grey pony.

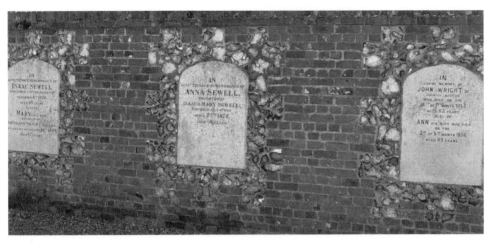

Graves of Anna Sewell and her family.

Recently, a rare collection of letters signed by Anna and dated from 1820 to 1860 are now back in Norfolk. In all, there are seven letters and a manuscript of a poem. One of the letters was signed 'your loving sister Anna Sewell' and others were signed 'Nannie', this being the family pet name for her.

Summers, Benanna (1825–1884)

Benanna came from Northrepps and was widowed at just twenty-five in 1850. Her jobs ranged from farmer and grocer to supporting her three children. The daughter of John Golden and his wife Elizabeth, she had been baptised on 17 January 1825. Her husband was a fisher driver called Edmund, whom she married on 12 January 1848.

By 1851 Benanna was farming 12 acres, and twenty years later she was a retired grocer still living in Northrepps with her son Edmund, a twenty-year-old carpenter.

In 1881 she was residing at Bulls Row, Northrepps, with her nephew Maurice Wagg and was employed as a laundress. She died in December 1884 and is buried at the local church.

Wadlow, Flo (1912–2013)

Florence Georgina Copeland was born on 8 December 1912 in West Ham, London. Her father, a Billingsgate fish porter, was killed in the First World War.

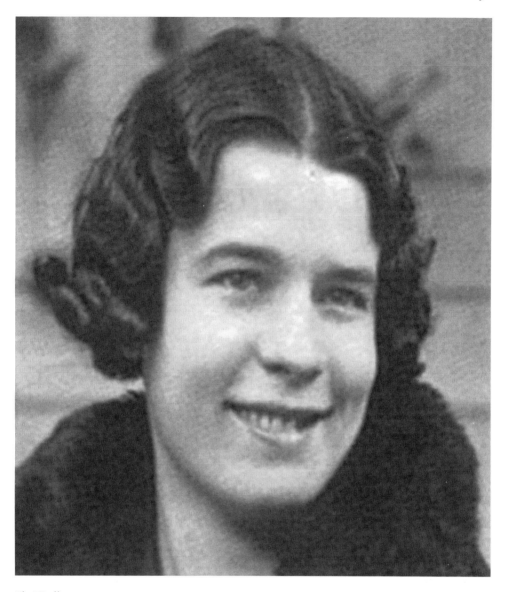

Flo Wadlow.

The family, including a younger brother, moved to Wells-next-the-Sea where her mother remarried and had a further three daughters.

Her life in service started at age sixteen, when she was a kitchen maid in South Kensington for a retired army officer and his two sisters for the sum of £20 a year. She was allowed a half-day off each week, every other Sunday off and a hot bath once a week. Flo gained experience at many houses before working at Mapleton in Kent for the sum of £30 per year. She gained more experience learning how to make pâté and soufflés. She left her position to work in Norfolk after contracting diphtheria.

Florence worked as a kitchen maid in the 1930s for the 4th Marquess of Salisbury at Hatfield House, Hertfordshire, who at the time was Leader of the House of Lords. Every morning the servants had to attend prayers. Flo only spoke with Lady Salisbury and never Lord Salisbury. Part of her position was to go with the family to their London House in Arlington Street, Piccadilly.

In 1936 Flo moved on to becoming a cook for the 11th Marquess of Lothian at Blickling Hall, who sent her to a technical college in Norwich to study elaborate puddings. By this time Flo was earning £50 a year.

Prime Minister Stanley Baldwin came to stay at Blickling during the Abdication Crisis in 1936. As they left after a three-week stay, Mrs Baldwin gave Flo £1 with a further £1 to be shared between the scullery and kitchen maid.

Flo left in 1939, when Lord Lothian became Ambassador in Washington, and she went to cook for the Bulwer-Long family at Heydon. In 1940 Flo married Robert Wadlow, who would be taken prisoner during the Second World War. The couple had two children and spent fifty years living in a cottage at Heydon before retiring to Fakenham in 1998. Robert died in 1983.

In 2004 BBC Radio 4 produced a programme about life in service which featured Flo. She also appeared in the TV series *Upper Crust* presented by Christopher Simon Sykes. Her memoir was called *Over a Hot Stove: A Kitchen Maid's Story.*

Flo was very dismissive of programmes such as *Upstairs Downstairs* and *Downton Abbey*, stating, 'They're not always true to how we used to be. They're how the programme makers think it was. They think they know it all, but they don't.'

Flo Wadlow died on 9 January 2013.

Wallace, Doreen (1897–1989)

Doreen was an author and a social reformer, born in Cumberland and educated in Malvern and Somerville College in Oxford. She went on to become a grammar school teacher in Diss, where she lived, before marrying Rowland Rash of Wortham, Suffolk, in 1922. They had three children.

Doreen went on to become a prolific writer and during the agricultural depression of the 1930s she campaigned against the imposition of tithes. This led to the impounding of stock on her two farms, which in turn led her to bankruptcy. She wrote a book about it called *The Tithe War*. Doreen was also involved in a siege when, in the mid-1930s, a train arrived in Diss with Hitler's and Oswald Mosley's Black Shirts, followed by a train with officers from the London Metropolitan Police.

In all Doreen had published fifty-four books from 1918 to the 1970s and was a member of the Somerville Group of writers that included Vera Britain and Dorothy L. Sayers. Her first novel was *Barnham Rectory*, which was published in 1934 and the last published was *Landscape with Figures* in 1976. Two years later she returned to live in Diss. She died on 22 October 1989.

Walne, Fanny (1828–1913)

Fanny was the daughter of a blacksmith and she was baptised in Litcham on 23 March 1828. Four years later her father passed away at the age of thirty-three and her mother took over the business.

Fanny was married on 19 October 1854 to Daniel Walne and between the years 1855 to 1869 they had nine children. Daniel could not have been a good businessman as he was declared bankrupt in 1865; he was also taken to court on numerous occasions for drunk driving, acquiring a horse under false pretences and smashing a window with a whip.

Fanny was given a family inheritance but was alarmed when in 1881 the funds were held back by her solicitor to pay some of Daniel's debts. In 1888 at a London court, Fanny sued her solicitor, saying that he had used £2,000 of her inheritance unlawfully, stating that she was made to sign a deed under severe pressure and thought that it was for a much smaller sum. Fanny won her case and the judge stated that the deed was wholly void, awarding Fanny the sum of £1,870 3s 4d plus costs, to be made available within twenty-four hours.

Women had just been given the rights to own property and money through the Married Woman's Property Acts of the 1870s, 1880s and 1890s, and it was through these acts that Fanny was able to stand up for her financial rights.

Daniel died in 1891 and not enough money was left for his funeral expenses. Fanny died in 1913 and is buried with Daniel at Pulham Market, in a family part of the churchyard.

St Withburga (d. 743)

St Withburga, who died in the year 743, was a princess, saint and abbess from East Anglia and the daughter of Anna of East Anglia. She founded a monastery at Dereham after her father's death and a traditional story states that, while Withburga was building the convent, she only had dry bread to give to those working on the site. After praying to the Virgin Mary she was

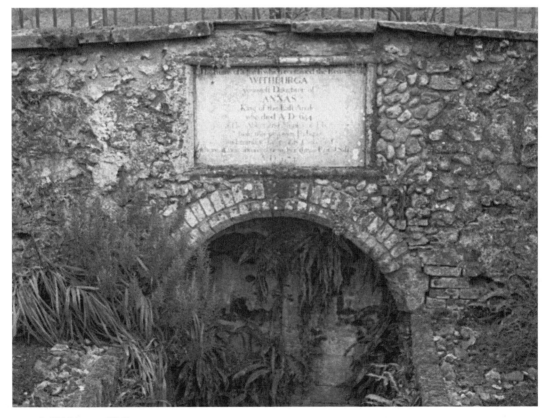

St Withburga Wall.

told to send her maids to the local well each morning, and there they found two wild does who they milked to give nourishment to the workers.

The local overseer was unhappy on hearing about these miracles and he hunted the does down with his dogs. He was punished for his doings by being thrown from his horse and breaking his neck. This story is commemorated by the town sign in the centre of East Dereham.

Withburga was buried in the cemetery at Ely Abbey and when her body was dug up some fifty-five years later, there showed to be no decaying. It was said to be a miracle and she was reinterred in the church that she built in Dereham, which became a place of pilgrimage.

Brithnoth, the abbot of Ely, set out to steal her body in the year 974 to profit from people visiting the tomb. A fight took place between the abbot's men and the men of Dereham. The Dereham men lost and Withburga was reinterred in Ely. When the men from Dereham returned to Withburga's empty tomb they discovered a spring and took this as a form of compensation. To this day the spring has never run dry and it can still be visited.

Zigomala, Hilda (1869–1946)

For nearly thirty years Hilda Zigomala (born Frances Hilda Keppel North) wrote about her family life in fifteen illustrated journals. Hilda, the daughter of Charles, a former deputy lieutenant of Norfolk, and Augusta North of Rougham Hall, was born on 29 July 1869. She started to collate her journals just after her wedding in St Mary's church, Rougham, in 1889. The tools that she used included pencils and watercolours, along with photographs highlighting her travels abroad with her husband, Major Pandia John Zigomala (often called Jack), which often included mixing with royalty.

The family started their life at Heath House in Farnham, Surrey, and from the years 1891 to 1896 they resided in India before moving to Egerton Gardens, London. They made many visits to stay at Rougham Hall and other established Norfolk houses, as well as Wroxton Abbey, Oxfordshire, the home of Lord North, and Ashtead Park, Surrey.

Hilda stopped writing after her fifteenth journal due to the untimely death of her only child, John, aged twenty-one, which took place just after the end of the First World War during the Russian Expedition.

All the journals bar one are now housed at the Norfolk Record Office. In the first volume Hilda talks about her honeymoon in Monte Carlo, having reached

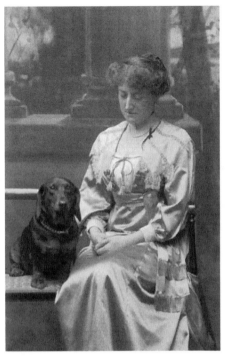

Left: Hilda Zigomala.

Below: Hilda Zigomala's wedding.

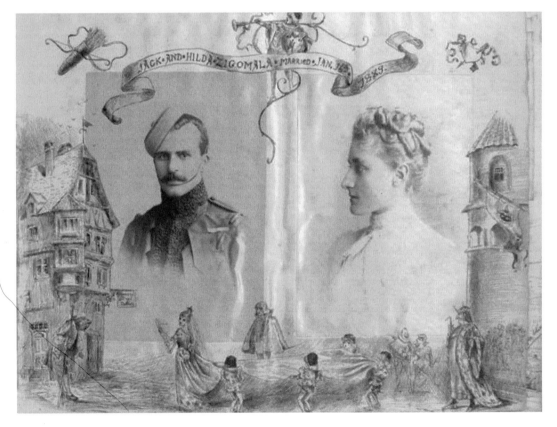

there via stopovers in London and Paris. Hilda writes about the birth of John in June 1898:

> At ¼ past five on Saturday afternoon the 11th June baby was born. I shall never forget the day, or that extraordinary feelings and sense of relief when it was all over and they brought me the young gentleman to see.

After John's death, Hilda threw herself into voluntary work. She taught crafts in Lord Roberts memorial workshops, which were set up for disabled former servicemen. Awarded the CBE in 1926, she was widowed in 1933 and died in London on 16 June 1946.

BIBLIOGRAPHY

Ball, Albert H. R., *Selections from the Paston Letters* (George G. Harrap & Co Ltd, 1949)

Bennett, Peggy D., *Sarah Glover: A Forgotten Pioneer in Music Education* (University of Texas)

Fenn, Ida, *Tales of a Countryman* (Geo. R. Reeve Ltd, 1976)

Marsden, Walter, *Resting Places in East Anglia* (Ian Henry Publications, 1987)

Smith-Dampier, J. L., *East Anglian Worthies* (Basil Blackwell, Oxford, 1949)

Tisdale, E. E. P., *Mrs Pimpernel Atkyns* (Jarrolds Publishers Ltd, London, 1965)

Also Available from Amberley Publishing

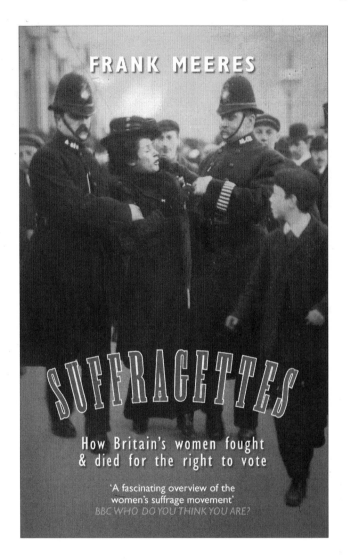

Paperback
192 pages
978-1-4456-3390-9

Available from all good bookshops or to order direct
please call **01453-847-800**
www.amberley-books.com